The purpose of this book is to document my running journey from start (first "official" 5k in 24:13) to current (sub 19:00 5k, sub 1:30 half marathon), along with the fun and interesting running knowledge I've picked up along the way.

Are you a reasonably in shape runner, and perhaps you've gotten your 5k time down to the 22:00-23:00 range with some training and general improved fitness? That's where I was. This book documents the steps I took to run more efficiently and further improve my running times. At some point I thought that it would be really cool if I could improve just a little bit more. I made it a goal to target the "magical" 20:00 5k barrier.

It took some hard work and dedication, but ultimately I achieved my goal. Is this something you want to target as well, and are perhaps confused by all of the available information out there? This book may help you, or at least demonstrate that "it can be done" (by the average runner)!

About the author (me):

I live in Michigan and enjoy the 9-10 months of the year where outdoor running is optimal. I consider myself an avid runner, although actual running only takes up 3-4 hours per week.

Profile:
Athlinks.com/athletes/82931515
E-mail:
joebee20min5k@gmail.com

Table of Contents

Forward

The purpose of this book is to document my running journey from start (first "official" 5k in 24:13) to current (sub 19:00 5k, sub 1:30 half marathon), along with the fun and interesting running knowledge I've picked up along the way.

Are you a reasonably in shape runner, and perhaps you've gotten your 5k time down to the 22:00-23:00 range with some training and general improved fitness? That's where I was. This book documents the steps I took to run more efficiently, and further improve my running times. At some point I thought that it would be really cool if I could improve just a little bit more. I made it a goal to target the "magical" 20:00 5k barrier.

It took some hard work and dedication, but ultimately I achieved my goal. Is this something you want to target as well, and are perhaps confused by all of the available information out there? This book may help you, or at least demonstrate that "it can be done" (by the average runner)!

Along the way, I've read a number of running books, and picked up various helpful hints and tips. In this book, I've shared what I have found the most useful for me. I've also added details of various races I've run over the years – how I've used the knowledge firsthand for improvements. This will help you see the steady progression I've made along the way. I will tell you in advance – there is no "easy" magic formula in this book. On the other hand, I am married with kids, and can't devote a ton of time to my running hobby.

So my recommendations do not include 35+ mile weeks of training either.
This book prescribes how given a decent starting point in terms of fitness and running ability...

- How to be efficient with your time
- Make the most of your abilities
- Gain a tremendous sense of accomplishment along the way.
- Have some fun!

Before taking up running, I did play sports fairly regularly and while I put on a solid 20 pounds from age 20 to my late 30's, I was in decent shape. Thus, this is not a "Couch to 5K book", rather a **Journey** from running 9:00 miles to running sub 6:30 miles. I have no natural "speed" talent, and however much I've tried **I cannot get under 15 seconds for a 100 meter run.** I was definitely not on any kind of track team in school, never won a short speed race and really just took up running as an activity in my late 30s.
My improvement has more to do with focus, endurance, and maintaining "decent" speed over periods of time ranging from 20 minutes to 2 hours.
Right now I am in my late 40s, probably in the best shape of my life (though I do thank God for general good health and steering me clear of accidental injuries), and about 20 pounds lighter than I was at age 20.

Running Habits (for me)

<u>(I'm just an average guy with not a lot of spare time)</u>

- I try to run 3-4 times a week, with weekly mileage usually around 20-25 miles.
- I enjoy running outdoors. I have limited "treadmill motivation". Remember, if you're outdoors there's more
  - Changing scenery
  - Motivation to run longer. Once you run "out" two miles, you pretty much need to run the two miles "back".

- I vary my runs by speed and distance. Based on the research I have done, I follow the training approach of using long, medium (faster) and short (fastest) runs (see Chapter 5). Also, by varying (and tracking) your runs, you keep them interesting and challenging.
- I wear a GPS watch (since 2013) and pay attention to it during the run. It's a "must" for meeting whatever race goal you set out to accomplish – whether a targeted 5k (see the 2014 notes on my first actual win), or knowing mid race whether you are on your planned half marathon pace. I definitely do a lot of math in my head while running. Also, see my 6/7/15 notes where I was successful in correcting the timing company!
- I will incorporate intervals (more frequently), and fartleks (occasionally).

- I generally "push the pace" at least once per week, which has a different meaning depending on how I feel and what the weather conditions are – don't try for a Personal Best (PB) half marathon when it's hot and humid!

- I incorporate some hills when I can. Some reasons:
  - "Shake things up", it's good to incorporate variety.
  - I look at hills as "quasi" Cross Training, given limited time to bike, swim, or do weights. However, experts would recommend actual biking, swimming, and weights.
  - To be better prepared for a hilly race experience – not let it affect my race.
  - Another way to build leg strength.

- Keep a running log and note the distance on my shoes – change them roughly every 500-600 miles. The industry recommendation is to change roughly every 300-500 miles, especially if you need the cushion. Of course, buy new ones well in advance (100-200 miles) just in case!

- I changed my running form substantially in 2012. I attribute a lot of incremental improvement to that change, and as a result am able to run longer distances with minimal leg pain. I have a couple of favorite running form videos that I like to share with others. See details in Chapter 5.

- I pay attention to hydration based on distance / temperature, especially after my June 2011 half marathon.

- I typically run in the morning – this is my strong preference as I don't have to worry about food settling in my stomach later in the day. Also, if you run first thing in the morning there's a smaller chance of something occurring to delay or cancel your plans!
- I run in the rain – actually it doesn't matter whether it's raining or not, if it's the right day to run I will be out there. See my 5/31/15 race notes!
- I read every running book I can get my hands on! I'm always interested in picking up helpful tidbits. As long as the books are written for the average runner, not for the elite ones!
- I am passionate about running and am willing to talk about and share all sorts of information with others. OK, sometime I'll share too much!
- I continue to set goals, improve my personal best times (see the table below).

The following table shows my average 5k and half marathon times since 2008. In some cases I've adjusted for what I believe are course length differences. I've also added the one constant race I've done every year since 2010, as a true "apples to apples" benchmark. That race is the Dexter to Ann Arbor half marathon, a somewhat hilly course usually run on the first Sunday in June. My time has improved from 1:43:10 in my first attempt in 2010 to slightly over 1:30 in 2016.

History: Average Race Times, Key Milestones

Average Race Times	5k *Average	Half Marathon *Average	Dexter Ann Arbor Half Marathon	Key Milestones During the year
2006-2007	27:00	N/A	N/A	Outdoor running
2008	24:13	N/A	N/A	I signed up for a 5k!
2009	22:00	N/A	N/A	Age Group "Win"
2010	N/A	1:40:00	1:43:10	First half marathon
2011	21:10	1:42:00	1:42:18	Longer training, pain!
2012	20:55	1:40:00	1:42:22	• Improved Running Form • Master's Title
2013 [a]	20:15	1:37:45	1:39:09	• "Unofficial" 5k under 20:00 • Improved overall Times
2014 [a]	19:35	1:33:00	1:35:02	• Official 5k under 20:00! • First Victory! • 10k Under 40:00
2015 [a]	19:15	1:31:30	1:33:18	• First Marathon • Sub 19:00 5k • Half Marathon under 1:30
2016			1:30:30	• 18:44 PB 5k

* Average adjusted for course length differences

[a] I consider years 2013-2015 the most significant in terms of improvement, as they were driven by more than just "fitness"

Running Habits (for others)

- Marathons: I've signed up and run one in 2015 just to say that I did it, but I didn't find it to be "fun". There's no question that it required a pretty substantial time commitment and preparation. I even (somewhat) qualified for Boston! I learned a lot from my experience, but that is another topic for another day... My key reasons for "not being as enthusiastic" about marathons include
  - The time commitment
  - You need an optimal time of the year to run one
  - In my personal experience, marathon training did not help me "get faster"

- Trail running – I mostly stick to pavement due to time restrictions, and actual proximity to trails (I am not close). However, I do stay off the roads avoiding the camber, and will stick to sidewalks whenever possible.

- Fast Running: As noted earlier I am not a "fast" short distance runner. Typical world class / Olympic winning time is typically under 10 seconds for 100 meters. College times are mid to low 10 seconds. Many athletes can run it in 12-13 seconds. If I really push it, <u>I can finish 100 meters in 15 seconds.</u> See Chapter 2, this is still running 15mph!

- I know that many others like to carry a phone or listen to music while running. If that motivates you, go for it! I personally don't. It's too much effort to carry the phone and keep in the headphones, and I enjoy the scenery.

- High(er) mileage: I've heard from others that say you need to put in 35-50 miles per week in order to drastically improve. I have found the right mix of workouts and intensity can be more beneficial than just running mile after mile without a plan. I don't run more than 3-4 times a week, as noted above, my mileage is usually at a maximum of 25-30 miles per week, rarely over 100 miles per month.
- "Two a days". While I have done this on occasion, there's not usually enough time in my day when accounting for showering, dressing, and "cool down" time to do this twice.
- I do not do much strength or cross training other than the hills I mentioned. I'll do hills once every 2-3 weeks or so just to remember "that they are there", though most experts will say this is not often enough to provide benefit. I will definitely do them more often if I have an upcoming hilly race. I have a desk job, and will do various leg and ankle stretches through the day (and of course have people wondering what the heck I am doing).
- Heart monitor: You'll need to make your own judgement on that one. It's probably something I should do but it's too much to think about. My GPS watch has time, distance, and pace and while it has the option for heart monitoring, I don't use that particular feature. It can be helpful in specific circumstances, and if you feel like there is any need from a medical perspective, consult a qualified physician! Many "old time" runners didn't use it either (Dave Scott, 6 time Ironman champion), but that doesn't prove anything.

- Stretching / Warm up: Definitely important, but I'm usually spending around a minute or two on this prior to a run, and another 1-2 minutes nightly on simple hamstring stretches. I won't start "cold" with a quick run, but that's about it. The jury is out on extensive pre exercise stretching. If it works for you, I definitely would not discourage it as it can be an important part of your training.
- Carb loading (prior to the race): For anything of half marathon distance or less, I haven't found the need to do this. For 10 miles or more, my maximum intake prior to a run is a half banana and half Cliff bar. I agree with carb loading for a marathon, but not important for a half marathon or less. Again, that is my personal opinion and experience but you need to do what works for you.
- While I prefer running outdoors, I won't run outside if it's under 20 degrees, or if there is ice and snow on the ground. In Michigan, this can be anytime from mid – November to mid – April! Basically, pick your days and use treadmills and indoor tracks as alternates.
- (Extensive) Traveling: For many, this is a source of motivation. You can even build a vacation around a run in another state or country. Until now however, I've been able to keep motivation pretty strong, as based on family and other obligations, I have not traveled more than about an hour to get to a race. Perhaps when I retire and the kids are married…

Why do I run?

#1: I actually enjoy it!

It's kept my weight stable after age 40, I feel great (most days) and have had minimal health issues.

It enables me to have a safe and energetic hobby – definitely a good alternative to car racing or online gaming.

I am a competitive guy (but aren't most guys competitive?), and it's fun to be in the top 5% of runners (even top 1-2%) in most races I run!

Socially – it's a great conversation piece, but be careful with non-runners as they may be totally uninterested.

1) The journey begins:

What was my starting point? This is difficult to pinpoint exactly…

Years: 2004-2006

I played basketball and other sports growing up and was in reasonably good shape. I had an old treadmill in the house that I would occasionally run on. My running was very sporadic, infrequent, and I never tracked my times / distances or set goals. I also did not vary my runs much by speed or distance. I remember that treadmill belt kept on shifting to one side or the other, and I had to constantly get off and reset it to the middle. I also owned one pair of high top athletic shoes which I used for basketball and then for running. Regardless, I could still get on the treadmill for 25-30 minutes and "crank out" 2-3 miles or so in the 9:00 – 9:30 pace range, but that was about it. Let's say I was able to run a 5k in the high 27 minute range…

Years: 2007-2008

Milestones:
- I purchased my first pair of "real" running shoes
- I moved from indoor to outdoor running

As basketball shoes are clearly not designed for running, I was developing blisters, along with a painful bunion.

I knew very little about running shoes, but at some point figured out that there were more and better options than running in the old high tops. I didn't know much about pronation or support options, I just figured I'd be prepared to spend $70-$100 on a pair of shoes. No bright colors or anything, just pick up "any pair that looked normal and was in my size". I lifted a pair and was amazed at how light they were, and how comfortable they were to wear. Of course the "gel" in the name made it sound even more exciting. Of course over time I've realized

- There's lot of options, based on level of running and running style
- All running shoe options were much lighter than high top basketball shoes!

One note on the bunions – make sure you get a second opinion when the recommendation is surgery! The first doctor (a surgeon) recommended some pretty extensive surgery, but my podiatrist took one look at it and said "this is going to hurt a lot, but by the time you leave here it will already start feeling better". Sure enough, about 15 (painful) minutes later his words were proven true. It was a mild bunion that just needed some scraping out.

Once the bunion was removed, I felt much more comfortable. I enjoyed running pain free in "real" running shoes, and literally added a change of scenery. We were doing some home construction and a result of clutter and various paint smells, I needed to get out of the house in order to exercise.

I started running outdoors and enjoyed it tremendously, as noted in my running habits. With the combination of running more frequently, and probably some stride adjustment from not worrying about falling off the treadmill, I found myself running an approximate 5k route in about 25 minutes. I then went out on a limb and signed up for my first race...

2) 2008-2009 Race Log and Topics

Date	Distance	Time	Personal Best?
10/19/08	5k	24:13	Of course! #1 motivator - Just sign up for something!
4/29/09	5k:	22:14	Yes, by almost 2:00
5/25/09	5k	22:03	Yes, by 0:11
10/18/09	5k	21:24	Yes, by 0:41

Date: October 19th, 2008

Race Name / Distance: Detroit Free Press / 5K

Race Result, Pace: 24:13, 7:45 Pace

Key Notes: First Race!

Details:

I signed up for my first official race in October 2008. It was the Detroit Free press marathon event, which draws approximately 20,000 participants each year. Folks travel from a number of states to participate, but the travelers are typically competing in the marathon and half marathon events. What makes these marathon and half marathon events special and unique is their international flavor and only "under water" mile. Runners run from the U.S. to Canada via the Ambassador bridge and back into the U.S.

through the Windsor tunnel, all within the first 8 miles. There is a beautiful view of the sunrise as you cross the Ambassador Bridge into Canada. Regardless, in 2008 I wasn't even dreaming about the half marathon, but just joining an event, the 5k. The 5k is run in downtown Detroit only. I would consider the day a success if I ran well, and didn't get too caught up in the emotions of my first run with such a large crowd.

The race started brisk and cold, but not too cold. These were actually pretty optimal race conditions. I did not have a GPS timing watch at the time, the race seemed to go on forever, and I vaguely remember thinking that the race was taking longer than expected. It was an amazing feeling to cross the finish line of my first race, the crowds lining the road give such motivation! I finished in 24:13, slightly under an 8 minute per mile pace. I looked at this as a tremendous accomplishment, knowing that the training I had put in had gotten me to this point. It also gave me confidence that it was something I was good at, and would actually be a "fun thing to do" in the future. It also answered the following question: Why do people enjoy running?

- It's a feeling of accomplishment, both for yourself and "for the record". There's a lot of personal satisfaction in seeing your official 5k time recorded somewhere, even if the only one who looks at it is you!
- Knowing there's always potential for improvement, whether longer distance or a faster time
- for those competitive folks out there, it's being able to be faster than others!

I was listed (in the local newspaper!) as 5th in my age group. The field was somewhat diluted however, as many strong runners would have been running in the marathon / half marathon events.

This race spurred me to make the decision to stick to the training – basically running between 1 and 3 times a week, but knowing that there was a certain time I was targeting. It helped to set a goal, the bar, and know that the results of my first race were a good starting point on which to build. My training was totally non-scientific and mostly indoor. I did some outdoor running as well and estimated the distance very roughly.

Between October 2008 and the following year, I attributed any improvement to simple repetition, general conditioning, losing some weight, and getting in better shape.
I signed up for a couple more 5ks in the first half of 2009.

Date: April 29, 2009

Race Name / Distance: Running Fit 5K

Race Result, Pace: 22:14, 7:10 Pace

Key Notes / Details: First "afternoon" race.

See my earlier note about preferring early morning runs, with a "settled stomach" as the primary reason. I was not impacted much at this race, but needed to carefully consider my "menu" throughout the day! In addition, as it was only my second race I was more nervous going in which probably contributed to "general queasiness".

Date: May 25th, 2009

Race Name / Distance: Grosse Isle Memorial Day 5K

Race Result, Pace: 22:03, 7:07 Pace

Key Notes / Details: Good way to celebrate Memorial Day! Lots of patriotism.

Once the warmer weather started, I set a target for myself. I would run the Free Press 5k again in October, but would target an "under 7:00" mile per minute pace.

Date: October 18th, 2009

Race Name / Distance: Detroit Free Press / 5K

Race Result, Pace: 21:24, 6:53 Pace

Key Notes / Details:

- Sub 7:00 pace for 5K!
- Age Group Winner!

Prior to mid-2010, I did not track my training runs. There was no scientific training for this race other than the "brute force" approach of running the same type of distance whenever I could, averaging two times a week. Again, nothing special about the training, other than I simply trained at a consistent level. I stuck to it and it paid off.

This was the first time I specifically tracked a targeted ending time. My goal was 21:42, which meant an average time under a 7:00 mile pace. When I got close to the finish and saw the clock at slightly over 21:00, I knew I had it! It's an amazing feeling, knowing that you "have your goal time in hand" and can almost chill out heading towards the finish. Of course, a good number of people will put on a burst of speed at the end in order to squeeze out every second of a personal best run. You can see it in their faces – no matter how long or difficult the race has been, they are looking to **"finish strong"**, and beat at least the person next to them, or gain a few extra seconds in the annals of history...

The other first I had in this race was "first" place in my age group! The race organizers are brilliant of course. In order to make you feel great about your race (and make you want to sign up again next year!) you are ranked against your age / gender group as well as overall. It's much better for you to hear that you finished 75th in your age group rather than 2000th overall. Also, the winners of each race (sometime up to 3 in each gender, and across regular and "masters" titles), are frequently not even counted in the age groups. In addition, for multi event races there are further splits by 5k, half marathon, full marathon, etc... As I mentioned earlier, typically there are higher caliber runners in the longer distances of multi-race events. If you've signed up for those longer distances you've probably done the training!

Thus, I ended up with an interesting result. As most of the "better" runners run the half marathon and marathon events, you can look relatively good if you run the 5k. There was only one person in my age group in the 5k with a faster overall pace, and he was the overall Masters champion with a time of 18:42 and didn't count in the age group standings! The results showed me as **#1 in my age group**, and I have the plaque to show for it! Again, I felt great about it at the time, and it continued to pique my interest in running. Some of this was luck of the draw of course, as to whom will sign up and what race they choose to run that year.

“Fast” – what does that mean, and how fast am I? How can I run 15 mph and still be slow?

If you appreciate “running math”, this chapter is for you.

Remember my time of 15 seconds for 100 meters.

This may seem slow to the average reader thinking about 100 meter times in the sub 10 second range for World class athletes.

However, average reader - think about your treadmill speed – are you “pushing it” at 9-10 MPH? Can you sustain it for 20 seconds? Congratulations! Your 10 MPH on the treadmill would be equivalent to a **22+ second 100 meter time**. Now do you realize how unattainable these times are? Olympic (and even College) sprinters with 11-12 second 100 meter times are in a totally different league. I can’t envision myself getting close to that!

Can you run 15mph? Does it seem difficult? My 15 second time for 100 meters is running at a pace of “only” 15 mph!!!

For reference:

Speed	Time it takes to run				Pace / Significance
MPH	1 Mile	¼ Mile	100 Meters	Marathon	
4	15:00	3:45	0:56	6:33:00	Brisk Walk
6	10:00	2:30	0:37	4:22:00	Decent Jog
8	7:30	1:53	0:28	3:16:30	Moderate run
9.33	6:26	1:37	0:24	2:48:33	20:00 5k speed
10	6:00	1:30	0:22	2:37:12	Top sustained speed over 30 seconds for most people
12	5:00	1:15	0:19	2:11:00	Top 10 marathon finish (In most major races)
12.8	4:42	1:10	0:18	2:02:57	Marathon World Record
14.7	4:04	1:01	0:15	1:46:40	5k World record (12:37)
15	4:00	1:00	0:15	1:44:48	4:00 mile (First done in 1954)
20	3:00	0:45	0:11	1:18:36	World class 400 meter time
22.5	2:40	0:40	0:10	1:09:52	World class 100 meter time

- 10mph: 1 Mile in 6 minutes, ¼ mile in 90 seconds, 100 meters in 22.5 seconds
- 15mph: **1 Mile in 4 minutes**, ¼ mile in 60 seconds, 100 meters in 15 seconds
- 20mph: 1 Mile in 3 minutes (The world record is 3:41, so this is pretty much impossible), **¼ mile in 45 seconds**, 100 meters in 11.25 seconds. This is close to a winning time for the 400 meter run in most international finals. The World

Record for 400 meters is 43:03 was set in the 2016 Olympics, more recent world championship runs are in the 44-45 second range).

22.5mph: 1 mile in 2:40 (again, for reference only but quite impossible). 400 meters in 40 seconds (a World record by a wide margin), **100 meters in 10 seconds**. Note this is **average** speed over the entire 100 meter distance, and does not include starting / stopping time. These guys are blazing fast, but remember that it still takes 1-2 seconds to get up to top speed. Thus, the top sprinters such as Usain Bolt are running a solid 23-24 mph for the last portion of the race.

You're now saying to yourself - OK – that makes sense. I'm not going to run 100 meters in 10 seconds, or run a 5 minute mile. How do I "get faster"?

You need to either

1) Increase your steps per minute over a prolonged distance (this is quite difficult)

and / or

2) Increase your distance per stride. This is somewhat attainable

It's quite simple, right?

Speed: Definition, and how to increase it!

Speed (S) = **Rate** (strides) per minute (R) x **Distance** per stride (D).

Let's reference as follows:
(R) Rate per minute.
(R) Rate per minute is also known as "Turnover speed" or "Cadence".

(D) Distance per stride = stride length

<u>(R) Rate per minute</u>
Most runners are running 160-180 steps per minute.

<u>(D) Distance per stride = stride length</u>
Most runners average between 3 and 5 feet per step. The simplest way to measure your stride length is to go to a track and see how many steps it takes to cover a 50 or 100 meter section. For example, say it takes 80 steps to cover 100 meters. This means that your stride length is 1.25 meters. Not bad – you're averaging approximately 4 feet per step!

<u>A Sample calculation</u> for speed is
1.25 meters per step (D) x 160 steps per minute (R) = 200 meters per minute, or 400 meters for 2 minutes **<u>if you can keep it up for 2 minutes.</u>** This is roughly an 8 minute per mile pace (**<u>if you can keep it up for 8 minutes</u>**), and about where I started when I did my first official 5k.

As mentioned, there are two "easy" ways to get faster, of course **assuming you can translate this into endurance** and over longer distances:

1) Increase your (R), Rate
2) Increase your (D), distance per stride

Endurance training will help keep up the speed over a longer period of time, but I have found that it's much harder to significantly increase R (Rate) than D (Distance per stride).

Let's get into this in a little more detail:

Increasing (R)

Most people will have diminishing returns on increasing turnover speed, as for longer distances it's pretty hard to get much over 180 steps per minute. However, there are several noted famous athletes that thrive on the high turnover, even over longer distances. (Over shorter distances such as 100 meters, you will see turnover in the 240+ steps per minute range.)

There are some benefits of increasing (R). For beginner runners, as you increase your cadence, your body will naturally gravitate towards proper running form. A faster rate / turnover (to some degree) forces a slightly shorter stride, so that feet stay underneath the body. This avoids "heel striking" which puts more stress on your legs and can lead to all types of injuries. Thus, with higher cadence, you tend to shorten your stride, stay light on your feet, and land in a better position.

Therefore, some improvement in cadence is helpful to improve running form, but as I have stated, for me the bigger speed pickup was from increasing stride length.

Increasing (D)

Where most improvement can be made is (D); distance per stride or stride length, by any of all of the methods below

a) increasing your leg strength through training and cross training
b) Running with improved form and using your strength and energy efficiently
c) Losing weight and using the same strength to propel your "lighter body" forward. My friend who is a personal trainer thinks highly of this last point!

Let's give an example using the table below, showing how a runner can improve his or her time significantly by improving stride length. I've chosen a half marathon distance, as for that distance you should be using consistent form, with long, easy, strides over an extended time period without trying for "speed".

(R) Rate per minute / cadence	(D) Distance per stride (feet)	Minutes per Mile	Half marathon time
175	3.50	8:37	1:52:58
175	3.75	8:03	1:45:32
175	4.00	7:33	1:38:59
175	4.25	7:06	1:33:05
175	4.50	6:42	1:27:50

As you can see from the table on the preceding page, increasing your stride length (while keeping everything else the same) can significantly improve your running times. Increasing stride length should be a natural result of continued exercise and building strength. While it may be more difficult to go from 3.5 feet to 4.5 feet per stride, you can see how increasing your stride a small amount, say 3.5 feet to 4.0 feet, can reduce your half marathon time by about 14 minutes.

How can I run 100 meters in 10 seconds?

Not to scare you, but let's now do the math on what it takes to run 100 meters in 10 seconds with a little bit of training...

22.5 mph

This is what you need to do!

100 meters in 10 seconds: 40 steps (4 steps per second) of 2.5 meters (roughly 8 feet!) each. (100 = 40 x 2.5)

The 2.5 meter stride length is pretty unattainable for the average human. Most of us can probably get to 2.5 meters in one jump, then fall over...

More reasonable: How can I run 100 meters in 15 seconds?

15 mph

Three sample options to get you there, but it's not easy!

60 steps in 15 seconds (240 turnover rate per minute) x 1.65 meter (5 feet) stride length. This is close to my personal estimate of how I "run it".

50 steps in 15 seconds (200 turnover rate per minute) x 2 meter (6.2 feet) stride length

45 steps in 15 seconds (180 turnover rate per minute) x 2.2 meter stride length – this one is much harder, as you need to get to 7 feet per step.

Overall, I hope this section helped break down the mechanics of what it means to "get faster". There's no magic formula, but over longer distances I'd say you need to concentrate on (D), as opposed to (R).

3) 2010 Race Log and Topics

Date	Distance	Time	Personal Best?
6/6/10	Half Marathon	1:43:10	Yes, First one!
8/31/10	8k	36:37	Yes, First one!
10/17/10	Half Marathon	1:37:28	Yes, by 5:40!

Date: June 6th, 2010

Race Name / Distance: Dexter to Ann Arbor run / Half Marathon

Race Result, Pace: 1:43:10, 7:52 Pace

Key Notes / Details:

- First Half Marathon!
- Not my "target" pace, but I didn't "bonk".

I followed a training program to get mileage in for my first half marathon. I generally followed one of the typical training programs, but learned that you can improvise, as long as you stick to the general theme of building up and tracking your mileage, and tapering off before the big event.

The event was in early June, and I worked with a 9 week program beginning in April.

The following was the official training program I followed.

"Official" Training Program for a Sunday race
For Saturday race, can move Sunday to Saturday, everything back one day

	SUN	MON	TUES	WED	THURS	FRI	SAT	Total
4-Apr	4		3		4	3		14
11-Apr	5		3		4	3		15
18-Apr	6		3		5	3		17
25-Apr	8		3		5	3		19
2-May	10		4		5	4		23
9-May	11		4		6	4		25
16-May	12		4		5	4		25
23-May	9		3		4	3		19
30-May	8		3		3	Walk 2		14
6-Jun	13.1							13.1

My training – generally tracked the recommended levels, but slightly lower.

Training I did for my first half marathon: the 2010 Dexter - Ann Arbor run

Actual	SUN	MON	TUES	WED	THURS	FRI	SAT	Total
4-Apr	5.5					4.0		9.5
11-Apr	6.8		3.1		3.1		4.0	17.0
18-Apr	5.7		3.1		4.9			13.7
25-Apr	3.1			8.3		4.0		15.4
2-May	10.0		3.9		6.0	3.0		22.9
9-May	11.3		3.1		5.5			19.8
16-May	12.3		3.1			4.1		19.5
23-May	9.9				6.0			15.9
30-May	8.0		4.0		2.6			14.6
6-Jun	13.1							13.1
13-Jun	6.1							6.1

Day of the race:

I remember the day being on the warm side but not excessively so. While I did not have a Garmin watch until 2013, there were clocks posted at each mile marker. I do remember with each passing mile feeling more and more behind my desired pace. I was targeting 1:40 and ended up at 1:43.

I realized after the fact that this was actually a pretty good result! I felt reasonably comfortable, I didn't panic, I still finished in the top 25% of runners in my event, and kept a sub 8:00 mile pace through 13 miles. However, this race was the first time I tried to hit a goal for a long term run and had just had the "sinking feeling" throughout. My lessons from this race it to stay within yourself and don't panic. The worst thing to do is to lose form as this can cause you to injure yourself. Also, stay hydrated! See my experience with the same race in 2011, where I did not concentrate on my hydration, did not track it, and paid the price.

Leg pain, injuries, new shoes, etc...

I discovered two pain issues around this time. One I was fortunately able to discover within a month or two, but unfortunately for the other one it took me two years to find and resolve. See my running form notes in Chapter 5.

First issue: Cambered Roads

As I started to run more than my usual 3-4 miles, I experienced increasing leg pain during the runs. At first this started to occur around 5 miles in to a run. Then it started earlier as I continued running, increased my mileage and took less rest between runs. I don't know exactly what made me figure out the issue. While I was running in the street, I was running on the side of the road instead of running in the middle or on the sidewalk. The issue was:

- **Cambered roads**: Since we have all been taught to run (or walk) against traffic, we tend to go to the left (in the U.S.) side of the street. This causes our left leg to be lower in relation to the opposite hip than our right, since roads have a slight angle or camber to help water drain off.

I found that even if you reverse yourself for the second half on the run by running on the other side on the way back, it doesn't take away the pain or damage to your legs. I don't know what advice to give folks that have no choice but to run on the side of the road. In general my advice would be to avoid sloped surfaces (where one leg is consistently higher than the other) as much as possible.

1) Run on the sidewalk – best option but watch for cracks!
2) run on trails or runner-only paths.
3) run in the middle of the road – pretty unlikely unless you're running at 4:00 AM before traffic hits

<u>Second issue: Bad Form</u>

– General soreness and stiffness after a run. It got to the point where I couldn't move much in the evening if I did a 4 mile run in the morning. I finally solved this by improving my running form, but this was not until two years later, in early 2012. My issue was mainly heel striking instead of mid-foot striking.

<u>Unrelated issue: Track your runs!</u>

Until early 2013, I did not use a device that accurately measured distance. I was measuring myself using some of the more popular websites such as MapMyRun. These are OK when following a straight course but not helpful for long runs with lots of turns, especially if you want to take shortcuts or vary your route vs. your original plan. You would need to stay on course, and cannot vary off to head down more interesting streets if you want to accurately track your distance!

Another issue: Accuracy! For some reason the MapmyRun distances were coming in 3-4% low compared to actual (as I discovered later). This was likely due to the measure assuming you're going in the street and not along a path of least distance such as an "inside sidewalk". This caused unrealistic expectations (and some mental anguish!) in a real race when you're hitting mile markers slower than expected.

With this introduction I can explain why in the June 2010 Dexter half marathon, I encountered a few issues

- First, it was a half marathon – I had never run that distance before! Time differences seem magnified, the race seems to go on forever, and you seem to be accomplishing less and less distance with every minute you look at the timing clocks on the side of the road. I was targeting a certain pace on a hot day, I didn't realize why I wasn't hitting my target timing, and I felt close to panicking...
- I didn't train for hills and while there were several smaller hills early in the race, I encountered a big one 7.5 miles into the run.
- I was still running on the side of the road, and my legs were in a lot of pain by the time the race was over.

August of 2010 is when I really got measured for running shoes….

This wasn't as big of a deal as I thought it would be – running stores are happy to help you and get you the right equipment, especially as they want you to be happy and keep on coming back. If needed, get two opinions but don't be afraid to try something new if you're comfortable with it. Most stores will do their best to satisfy you, and will let you take a product home or at the very least try it out for some treadmill running. There's also all sorts of accessories (for all sorts of weather) they would like to sell you! They want to become your consultants and help you through every step.

Personally, I had run with ASICS the first few years and as I mentioned they were a tremendous step up from my old basketball shoes. I went to Running Fit - a great chain of stores in Southeast MI - and learned that I was a mild over pronator. I was shown two pairs of shoes, ASICS and a pair of Mizunos. The ASICS were what I was used to and comfortable with. The Mizunos just felt very comfortable and light. Looking back on it, it should have been an easy decision to switch. However, most people have the inherent nature of being resistant to change. Fortunately, in this case I overcame my resistance and got the Mizunos for the comfort. They just felt so much lighter and less restrictive around my foot, even though the sole and ground "strike" felt similar between them.

Again, just try a few brands and find ones that work best for you. Don't be afraid to try something new, but not on race day!

Date: August 31st, 2010

Race Name / Distance: Grand Prix Shakedown, 8k

Race Result, Pace: 36:37, 7:19 Pace

Key Notes / Details:

- First 8k
- Ability to recognize a different pace for "middle distance" runs.

Date: October 17th, 2010

Race Name / Distance: Detroit Free Press, Half Marathon

Race Result, Pace: 1:37:28, 7:26 Pace

Key Notes / Details:

- Nice time overall, but bad pacing contributed to an injury

First (and fortunately so far only) injury

I signed up for the Free Press half marathon later in 2010 and trained a lot less than I did for the Dexter run. I somehow pulled off a 1:37:28 finish. I started way too fast. Based on the chip timing (which is not always accurate mid-course), I completed 10k in 44 min or slightly over 7:00 per mile pace. I really struggled to finish. I probably didn't hydrate enough but got away with it because of the cooler weather. It seemed like every single part of my legs were sore for the next couple of days, more so than I had ever experienced on a long run. In my mind, this was caused by two clear factors:

A) Bad running form, which impacted my ankles, knees, etc…
B) Once you get tired and push to finish a race, you're not going to run with good form. As a result you will be "forcing" yourself to take thousands of steps of repetitive pounding the pavement, likely not using your natural stride.

I must have done something to my meniscus, as when I tried to play basketball a week later something popped and I couldn't run for 3-4 weeks without pain, and kept on injuring it every time I jumped. I needed to pretty much take time off from running for 2 months, from November – December until I was back to being "somewhat pain free".

I learned that

- While running is not a contact sport, it is considered a high impact sport because of the ground forces up to 2.5 times your body weight on impact. It's easy to get injured – repeated stress on a joint will do that and you need to minimize it as much as possible.
- No one is indestructible – if your body is telling you something hurts you should be paying attention to it.
- You sometimes just need time to recover from an injury
- Running form really matters - if you have good form it enables longer running with less pain. There is an April 2012 New York Times article that discussed a study

done on Harvard University's distance running teams. The data showed that while two thirds of the group wound up hurt enough to miss two or more training days, heel strikers were much more prone to injury, with a twofold greater risk than the forefoot strikers.

- Age matters – be more careful as you get older

There's a lot of places to look up running injuries, and many different exercises and methods to treat each one! Once you figure out what injury you have – which may require at least one visit to a sports medicine doctor, you can almost always get lots of second opinions on the internet as to how to treat the injury. The best advice I got - from a sports medicine doctor - is that you should avoid surgery whenever possible. Rehab and exercise are the best way to get the joints and muscles back to their original shape.

I'm definitely not the expert on this, but if you're getting into running and looking for pre-emptive moves to avoid injury, here are some things to look into:

- Specific exercises for building running strength
- Foam Rolling, mostly post exercise
- Yoga – full body fitness and strengthening

4) 2011 Race Log and Topics

Date	Distance	Time	Personal Best? / other notes
5/4/11	5k	20:33	No, as likely shorter than 5k
5/30/11	8k	35:37	Yes, By 1:00
6/5/11	Half	1:42:18	Hydration issues!
8/21/11	10k	46:01	Yes, first 10k!
8/30/11	8k	34:58	Yes, by 0:39
9/18/11	10k	43:50	Yes, by 2:11
10/16/11	5k	21:09	Yes, by 0:15

Date: May 4th, 2011

Race Name / Distance: Running Fit / 5k

Race Result, Pace: 20:33, (* 7:00?) Pace

Key Notes / Details:

* Was likely less than 3.1 miles.

Date: May 30th, 2011

Race Name / Distance: Grosse Isle / 8k

Race Result, Pace: 35:37, 7:07 Pace

Key Notes / Details:

8k PB by one minute

Heat / Hydration

Date: June 5th, 2011

Race Name / Distance: Dexter to Ann Arbor run / Half Marathon

Race Result, Pace: 1:42:18, 7:48 Pace

Key Notes / Details: I didn't hydrate properly, and paid for it!

My finish time may seem like an OK result, but I would qualify it as my worst race ever, and I hope this never happens to anyone!

This run was before I started carrying hydration bottles with me, and it was brutally hot and humid that day. I actually don't remember too much of this race after mile 10. I do remember grabbing some water at the stations, but don't remember how much I actually drank from each cup before tossing it to the side. I do remember

- Becoming more and more frustrated as the race went on, as I was not hitting my target pace
- Thinking "I just want to get over this", and I kept on pushing to finish
- Not being used to "drinking on the run" from a cup, so I don't know how much I actually drank..
- Things got blurry in the last mile and I only vaguely remembered the finish line
- Not much after that until waking up in the hospital

I was told I needed to be transported in an ambulance and they were genuinely afraid of what had happened to me. I was likely out cold for about 30 minutes and have much to be grateful for - there was no significant damage other than heatstroke (and a decent sized hospital bill).

Most important lesson! Stay hydrated! You can hurt yourself by overdrinking (mostly after a race, but sometimes during a long race as well) but can hurt yourself more by not drinking enough. Go slow and walk if you're really having a hard time – you can't hit your goals every day, and there's always another race. You should learn how to drink on the run so that you don't lose time, but more important you actually drink something without spilling most of it out!

My rule of thumb has been that for distances of 8 miles or more, you really need to track your fluid intake, and it will vary based on the weather and based on your history and experience. For runs of 45-50 minutes or less, if you're hydrated well beforehand it's usually fine to grab 4-8 ounces through the run. If it's hotter, go towards 8 ounces which is the equivalent of two cups at aid stations. As these cups are usually half filled, expect 3-5 ounces in the cup, you might get 2-4 ounces after accounting for sloshing / spillage. Drinking 8 ounces at one station may be too much, and could impact your stomach.

Most important for hydration / nutrition – everyone will tell you this. <u>Follow the same conditions in the race that you follow in practice, and don't try anything new for the race.</u>

Other 2011 Milestones

I had more consistent training, better fitness, similar to my approach for 2008-2010 and the early part of 2011. This improved my times a bit more, to slightly above a 21:00 5k by the end of the year, but I felt like this was pretty much my limit. I wasn't getter much faster, I had constant pain after running, and I seemed to be "hitting my max potential".

Date: August 21st, 2011

Race Name / Distance: Running the Rails Ypsilanti / 10k

Race Result, Pace: 46:01, 7:24 Pace

Key Notes / Details: First 10k!

Date: August 30th, 2011

Race Name / Distance: Grand Prix "Shakedown" / 8k

Race Result, Pace: 34:58, 6:59 Pace

Key Notes / Details: 8k under 7:00 pace!

Date: September 18th, 2011

Race Name / Distance: Run Wild at the Detroit Zoo / 10k

Race Result, Pace: 43:50, 7:03 Pace

Key Notes / Details: 10k PB by 2+ minutes

Date: October 16th, 2011

Race Name / Distance: Detroit Free Press / 5k

Race Result, Pace: 21:09, 6:49 Pace

Key Notes / Details: PB, but knew it would still take a lot of work to get to sub 20:00!

I felt I was at peak form for this race and did pretty well, but was only 15 seconds faster than my time in 2009. Thus, my uncertainty in being able to achieve additional improvement.

VO_2 Max and Lactate threshold (Simplifying)

Why am I including this section? There is a lot of scientific research into what drives improvement. I've read a lot about this, and I've gotten a basic understanding. I've condensed what I know below. You never know when you can use good, intelligent sounding information at a dinner party!

Increasing **VO_2 Max** enables you to maintain high intensity for (relatively) shorter races such as 5k and 10k distances.

For longer races (generally more than 100-120 minutes), you will benefit by improving your **lactate threshold**.

VO_2 Max:
VO_2 max is a measure of the maximum volume of oxygen that an athlete can use.

The general concept is;

As you increase your effort when you exercise, the amount of oxygen you consume to produce energy (and hence the rate at which you exhale carbon dioxide) increases. However, there is a maximum level of oxygen consumption, which does not increase with further increases in exercise intensity. This level of oxygen consumption is called the VO_2 max. (The initials simply stand for Volume of Oxygen.)
Some experts believe that VO_2 max is a key physiological determinant of an athlete's running performance, and that

it is an important objective of a training program to improve it.

Your VO_2 max is to a large extent determined by your genes; but it can be increased by training. Studies have shown that most people can increase their VO_2 max by between 5% and 20% through training.

Based on the various materials I have read, one of the key methods in increasing VO_2 max is running shorter, high intensity runs with small breaks in between. Namely, some of what I did "inadvertently" through interval training, to a large degree helped in maintaining higher levels of speed for medium distances of 5k-10k.

Lactate Threshold: If you increase your lactate threshold, you can exercise at higher intensity for longer periods of time without increasing blood lactate levels.

The lactate threshold is the level of exercise above which lactate is produced faster than it can be removed (metabolized) in the muscle.

Above this level of exercise intensity, blood concentration of lactate and / or lactate acid begins to increase. Increased lactate levels will result in **decreased** muscle contraction capacity and ultimately in performance.

Below this level of exercise intensity any lactate produced by the muscles is removed by the body without letting it build up. There will be **no** performance decline.

Improvements in lactate threshold: Regular endurance exercise leads to adaptations in the muscles which for a given level of intensity, will prevent lactate levels from rising.

5) 2012 Race Log and Topics

Date	Distance	Time	Personal Best?
4/22/12	Half	1:44:15	
5/29/12	5k	21:38	
6/3/12	Half	1:42:22	
6/24/12	5k	21:11	
8/12/12	5k	20:39	Yes, by 0:30, but may have been <5k distance
10/21/12	Half	1:39:08	
11/22/12	10k	43:27	Yes, by 0:23

My main accomplishments in 2012:

- I transformed my running form and felt a ton better
- I was able to maintain a good level of training – was able to run more with less pain
- I started concentrating on intervals and speed work
- I set one personal best and got close on several others
- I won a Master's title!
- I finished strong in all my races
- I started thinking (and reading) about what it would take to achieve a 20:00 5k time.

Running Form

As this was a topic of interest for me, I started to read running books in my spare time. As I kept reading about proper form (which I pretty much ignored my first few years of running) I realized that "the concept existed and I wasn't following it".

Around April of 2012, I watched one of the most helpful videos I have ever seen. The video I saw showed someone running on a track with two different running form / styles. The first style looked totally normal to me at first, while the second style looked very awkward. The video then takes apart each of the runs in slow motion, showing how the second style is more efficient, and more important significantly reduces the level of stress on your joints.

You can find the Youtube video, "Pose Running clinic (Before and after) by Posecoach Jacky"

Key messages:

- You should "pick up" your feet and come down straight underneath your body. This is much preferred to coming down at an angle where your foot hits the ground "in front" of your body.
- Think of a "circle" or "wheel" where the foot is placed down and almost instantly used to push forward to the next step. Again, intentionally picking "up" your foot with each step, bringing it down flat, and pushing forward as you are coming down. The best way I can describe it is "bicycle form" as you are essentially riding

a bike. Your feet should be coming down and pushing forward, minimizing impact and braking.

- Avoid heel striking, which also adds "braking" with each step along with joint stress. Heel striking requires more support, which results in wasted energy and (potentially) lower cadence.
- Keep rate / cadence close to 180 steps per minute, this will minimize the required support from your joints. See my earlier notes on how increasing (R) will improve running form.
- Optimum landing position is on the middle of the foot (slightly behind the ball of the foot), or at least evenly across the whole foot.
- Body posture is important, with alignment of hips, shoulders, and feet.

Here's a picture of me in the last mile of the 2015 Detroit half marathon, you can see some of what I am referring to…

My advice: Do whatever you can to improve form, increase efficiency, and minimize injury. Do this either through professional stride analysis or figuring this out yourself through research as I did.

Some running stores will do stride analysis for free, or have clinics (of course to get you in the door and buy something). While it may take a bit of time to “re-align” your stride, it shouldn’t be more than 2-3 weeks and it’s well worth it in the “long run” (pun intended).

Other important considerations:

Can you keep the form all the way through a long run, no matter how tired you are? This will help avoid injury from repetitive stress.

The more you run efficiently and the more comfortable you get with your form, you will build leg strength in the right places. This will likely increase stride length as I mentioned earlier – notes on increasing (D) or distance per stride.

Race Pacing

Date: May 29th, 2012

Race Name / Distance: Grand Prix Shakedown / 5k

Race Result, Pace: 21:38, 6:59 Pace

Key Notes / Details:

I participated in a race with a couple of co-workers, "Mike" and Doug.

In general, a good percentage of runners are not disciplined self-pacers, and have the tendency to fly out of the gate. I see way too many runners starting too strong, and then fading behind me as the race goes on. It never seems like anyone else is running hard at the beginning, but trust me if you are all training at the same pace and others start faster, they are working harder than you and will pay for it later.

This particular race was a late afternoon 5k. It was late May, but the weather already felt like mid-summer. It was in the high 80s and humid, definitely the kind of race where

- you would not be targeting your PB
- You will definitely suffer later in the race if you start too fast. Stay within yourself, can always pick it up halfway through. You don't know how rewarding it is to do so and pass early leaders later in the race

- It's not really a long enough race to cause mid race hydration issues, assuming of course you are healthy, drank before the race, and are used to running a 5k without hydration.

The most important message is – **run at your own pace and don't let the pace <u>others</u> run dictate <u>your</u> pace**, especially in the first mile! I will continue to stress this point throughout the book, but I feel it's totally important in maximizing race performance. You can train superbly for a race but lose all the benefit of that training because of poor pacing.

Mike started way ahead, and had an approximate 20+ second lead after the first mile. You will learn that while a 20 second early lead looks big when you are behind, you need to remember to run your own race and see if they come back to you. 20 seconds is actually easy to make up if your competition goes out too fast. If they are really pacing themselves well and are 20 seconds ahead, **<u>there's not a whole lot you can do anyway, they are just faster than you</u>**! Take the scenario on the following page where both runners train at roughly a 7:00 pace over a 5k distance:

Pace per Mile	Undisciplined runner ("Mike")	Joe	Joe: overall status
Mile 1	6:35 (pushes the pace, gets caught in the moment)	7:00	25 seconds behind
Mile 2	7:10	7:00	15 seconds behind
Mile 3	7:25 (tiring)	6:55	15 seconds ahead
Mile 3.1	0:50	0:45	20 seconds ahead
Total Above	21:50	21:40	20 seconds ahead

Whom do you think can pick it up in the last quarter mile? Whom do you think feels better after the race?

The scenario played out almost exactly as above. Mike continued to lead through the first mile, and even through most of the second mile. Doug was 10 seconds ahead of me and 10 seconds behind Mike. Neither saw me. I kept on with my level pace, no one was passing me and I was staying pretty level with the others. About 2.5 miles in, Mike started to "come back" to Doug and me. I noticed that the gap was closing, and Doug was getting much closer to Mike. Doug caught Mike and passed him, then I did the same to Doug. Mike was pretty much done, and not able to respond. This is typical when you expend energy early in the race, get exhausted later, and people start passing you. Meanwhile, Doug was probably feeling pretty good. He was setting a nice pace, and had just passed a pretty strong runner he had been trailing most of the race.

I felt like at this point it was all or nothing. It was pretty hot, but with only a half mile to go you can sort of let it hang out and just go for it. I went ahead and pushed the pace a bit to pass Doug. I wasn't sure how he would respond, but know I was close to my limit as well. My goal was to at least keep the strong pace for the 10 seconds or so after passing Doug, and then level off and hope he wouldn't be able to close the gap himself.

Final standings in the 5k (the three of us finished among many other finishers):

21:38: Joe
21:49: Doug
22:00: Mike

Remember, it was hot and humid, and while I had run faster times I thought the 21:38 was a pretty good performance. I was still thinking along the lines of "OK, perhaps I should do about a minute better with cool conditions" (20 seconds per mile), but there's still a **huge** difference between 21:38 (6:59 pace per mile) and 20:00 (6:25 per mile).

What's the big deal about a 20:00 5k?

Somehow I got very interested in the "magical" 20:00 barrier. For me, this became a big deal, and something I really wanted to set out to accomplish.
As with any running goal, once you do it and your time is "published" it's something that no one can ever take away from you.

For non-elite athletes (I definitely qualify as non-elite!), some other "magical" barriers include goals along the lines of a 6:00, 7:00, or even an 8:00 mile, a 20:00, 25:00, or 30:00 5k, and a sub 3:30 / 4:00 marathon.

At an elite level, this might look like: 10 seconds for 100 meters, 4:00 for a mile, 13:30 for a 5k, or a sub 2:15 marathon...

Of course, there are a couple of reasons why it's easier to go from 24:00 (7:45 pace) to 22:00 (7:05 pace) than 22:00 all the way down to 20:00 (6:26 pace).

1) Simple math: There is a law of diminishing returns to training. Getting closer to a fixed limit (say a world record at a 4:05 pace or even a more realistic limit of a 6:00-6:15 pace) gets progressively harder the closer you get to it!

2) Specific steps you've already taken, such as improved running form and weight loss are no longer options to take advantage of, as you've already taken those steps and need to come up with new ones!

Date: June 3rd, 2012

Race Name / Distance: Dexter to Ann Arbor run / Half Marathon

Race Result, Pace: 1:42:22, 7:49 Pace

Key Notes / Details: What a (major) difference a year makes!

Based on the prior year's performance I had good reason to be nervous about the race and took precautions. I had purchased my hydration belt and was generally in much better shape. I planned for how I needed to space out my drinking at each stage of the race.

I could have probably gone out harder in this race, but I actually tried to be stay purposely steady, and pay attention to what my body was telling me. I remember the race being pretty hot, but uneventful **all the way to the end.** For me, this was a very successful race – I accomplished a very solid time, felt comfortable and in control the whole way through, finished strong, and while it certainly required effort I felt really good about the race.

Thus, it was only 4 seconds off vs. 2011, but as different as night and day.

My Training Method: Long, medium, & short runs

I noted in the Introduction that I follow the training approach using long, medium (faster) and short (fastest) runs.

Here are some basic facts:

You need all 3 types of runs to increase speed and endurance.

- Longer runs should be at an easy, comfortable, pace, during which you should be able to carry on a conversation.
- Medium runs: should be slightly uncomfortable
- Shorter runs or intervals at a more difficult pace.

Not more than one long run per week.
Try and "push the pace" on one of your runs once a week.

I will show / illustrate

- How you can accomplish this mix of speed and distance with anywhere from 20-30 miles per week
- The specific pace you would target in order to ultimately achieve a sub 20:00 5k.

If you want to target a 20 minute 5k, here's what you need to get to, it's as simple as this (and may be the most important part of the book):

Can you build yourself up to the following goal?

****

8-10 intervals of 86-90 second 400 meter runs. In between intervals, take short walking or light jogging breaks of 75 to 90 seconds.

****

If you can accomplish the above, it's likely you will be able to run a sub 20:00 5k.

Can you run **one** 400 meter interval at anywhere close to 1:30? If so, you can get to this level over time if you continue to work at it. It definitely won't happen overnight. Try for 1 interval, then 2 intervals with a 5 minute break, then 3 with 3 minute breaks, etc...

If you are targeting a slower pace than the 20:00 5k, do the same pattern but with slower (i.e. 1:45 or 2:00) intervals.

You will need the mix of short, medium, and long runs in order to accomplish this.

Let's do some basic math. In order to run a 20 minute 5K you need to average 1:36 per quarter mile (6:26 pace per mile) over the entire distance. Running 1:26-1:30 in training with short breaks, along with longer runs at slightly slower speeds (say roughly 1:45 per mile or 7:00 per mile pace), will enable and train your body to achieve the target of a 400 meter 1:36 pace for 20 minutes.

Details - my specific training targets:

The training times below target a 20:00 5k run, but can also get you to a half marathon time close to 90 minutes. While reading this section, consider the following: "Am I really committed to doing this, and willing to put in the work in order to ultimately be successful?"

A) Long Runs

Target

Time: 60-105 minutes
Speed: 6:50-7:20 pace per mile
Distance: 9-13 miles.

Goals = Strength and endurance, aerobic conditioning.
I typically do not target more than this distance or time.

Note: This is actually faster than what many would recommend for a long run given the 86-90 second target 400 meters. I've read that the longer runs should be 60-90 seconds slower than race pace, which would mean a 7:30-8:00 pace for long runs. My recommendation above is about 20-45 seconds above my 10k race pace. Again, it's worked for me but others "swear by" a much slower pace for long runs. (I personally just can't get comfortable at too slow of a pace!)

I target at least 8-9 miles once a week, with 11—13 miles once or twice a month.
Stay at a steady pace, keeping the pace for the entire distance.
If you are in good shape, you can miss this run occasionally. If you need the rest, or reduce the mileage, that's OK. You can do the "medium runs only" one week (skip the long runs), by keeping the slower pace for a short distance.

Again, these are solid, steady runs, and your speed can vary somewhat. Thus, they can be anywhere from 6:50 to 7:20 pace, typically faster pace for shorter distances within this range.

B) Medium / Tempo Runs

Target
Time: 40-65 minutes
Speed: 6:45-7:05 pace per mile
Distance: 6-9 miles.

These runs accomplish the goals of both the long and short runs. They build endurance, and you don't have to be out for more than an hour! They increase your endurance, and aren't a major time investment.

These should be solid, steady runs, at slightly faster than your "long run" pace. You can have vary your speeds by +/-20 seconds per mile. You can include fartleks (see below!) of a quarter mile to as long as 1 mile. If you do the mile

fartlek, use the next mile as a recovery and go slower than your planned average, otherwise it will be hard to maintain.
If there is an opportunity to run on a hilly portion for part of the run, take the opportunity. There is no need to force the pace on the hill though.

C) Short Runs or Intervals

This follows the logic in the famous quote - **"You need to run faster in order to run faster!"**

C1) Short Runs

Target
Time: 20-45 minutes
Speed: 6:05-6:30 pace per mile
Distance: 3-5 miles.

C2) Intervals

Target
Time: 20-45 minutes
Speed: 6:00 or less per mile (during the "speed" portion)
Distance: 2.5 - 4 miles of "speed" running. The total distance will be more when including cooldown (light jog or walking) time.

Short runs are crucial. Short runs at high speed make it much easier to run longer runs at slower speeds. For example, if you can run 400 meters in 1:30, it should be less difficult to run 800 meters in 3:30. If short runs are done consistently and you get used to the faster speed, it makes your longer & slower runs seem like gentle jogs!

Goal: Run faster, build speed / improve recovery.

As noted, intervals would total 2.5 - 4 miles of speed work, so it could be a trial 5k, or 8-10 intervals of 400 meters with breaks in between. Try and do one of these once per week, if you want to keep improving.
Use either shorter distances at higher intensity, or a single run at high speed, or some combination of the above in order to get to the total of 2.5 – 4 miles of "hard" running.

Note: For 5k races, usually an athlete does not run the race distance at race speed during training. I typically try to do so, but it can be hard on the body so again, see what works for you.

Short runs improve running economy, running speed (of course!) and max **VO_2**.

This is the one type of run where I warm up first! Don't jump right into a quick 400 meters. Start with stretching or light jogging (a couple of times around the track) until you are comfortable enough to begin.

My Interval target (noted above in the 20:00 5k goals): 400 meters; 8-10 repetitions at 1:26 to 1:30. Alternately, a "quick 5k" in the 20:00-21:00 minute range.

With intervals, try to be as consistent as possible. Thus, even though you might be able to run a single lap of 400 meters at 1:20 or below, it will throw off the training as it will require recovery and ultimately less repetitions. Of course, it's OK to go all out on the last interval in your set...

The repetitive nature and relatively short recovery will build endurance for slightly slower sustained runs. The 86-90 second 400s with short breaks will enable the 96 second 400s for a full 5k.

You can also go "all out" with 100 or 200 meter runs, along with breaks in between. For these **really** short runs, you will need to push yourself to move your limbs faster. Specifically, for runs of 20 seconds or less you should target 40 strides per 10 seconds (that's a rate of 240 strides per minute).

Intervals, Fartleks, Ladders, Stride Outs

Intervals:

Intervals are short, quick runs, with brief breaks of light jogging or walking in between. Most of my comments on intervals are already captured above.

My targets Intervals:

400s (more frequently) or 800s (once in a while):

400 meters (as noted above); 8-10 repetitions at 1:26 to 1:30. 5:45-6:00 per mile pace.

800 Meters: 5-8 repetitions at 2:58 – 3:05. 5:55-6:10 mile pace.

You should take walking breaks between intervals, or slow jogs. My goal was always to "keep moving" between intervals, and keep the breaks between 75-90 seconds, perhaps 90-120 seconds for the 800 repeats.

Fartleks

Fartlek means "speed play" in Swedish, is a training method that blends continuous training with interval training. Fartlek training is simply defined as "periods of fast running intermixed with periods of slower running." Fartleks are unstructured and alternates moderate-to-hard efforts with easy throughout the run. After a warmup, you run at faster efforts for short periods of time (to that tree, to the sign) followed by easy-effort running to recover. I believe this trains your body (and provides mental support) that you can vary speeds during a race, expend energy at different levels, and not lose your focus and overall endurance.

Ladder workouts:

Ladder workouts are speed sessions that vary the length of the work intervals in incremental steps. You can get a mix of several high-intensity running paces in a single session. Go to the track, and after warm ups try the following.

Basic ladder: 1600 meters, 1200, 800, 400.
Run each interval slightly faster than the preceding one, and jog 400 meters between each interval.

There is a lot of material online to read on this topic, there's not much I can add.

I generally rely on fartleks as my "change of pace" runs. I have not done "concentrated" ladder workouts as part of my regular training, but I have usually mixed in some 800s and 200s in my interval training.

Others feel this is an important part of their workout, thus the saying "do whatever works best for you"!

Stride outs:

Stride outs are 60- to 100-meter "pickups" that runners typically do just before speedwork or races. In these instances, runners generally warm up well, stretch, and then use strides as a finishing touch to ease into fast-running mode. You do strides before a bout of fast running to do the following: muscles need to be flooded with blood, race pace is briefly simulated to get the body and mind ready to run fast.

The theory is that stride outs also improve your neuromuscular coordination, as the bursts of speed stimulate neural pathways. Your coordination and form become more fluid from these short but frequent doses of speed tacked onto the ends of easy runs. Result: You become faster.

I do a couple of forms of Stride outs, depending on the occasion:

A) Pre race: Before running a 5k, I will always run a quick 5-10 second burst of speed at "faster than race pace", close to top speed. I find this helps my brain register that my 5k pace is sustainable over the 20 minutes, as I just ran something much faster, albeit over a much shorter distance...

B) End of race: I just like finishing strong (though this may just be driven by my ego?)...

Masters Title!

Date: June 24th, 2012

Race Name / Distance: Scleroderma / 5k

Race Result, Pace: 21:12, 6:50 Pace

Key Notes / Details:

This was another first for me. While I had won my age group in the past, this was the first

- Master's title
- Prize money award

Is this 5K race, I remember passing an older guy (another 40+ age) with about a half mile to go and didn't think much of it at the time. Sometime mid- afternoon I got a call from the race director asking me to "pick up my prize". It was a $50 gift certificate, but it felt pretty special.

Date: August 12th, 2012

Race Name / Distance: Milford Memories / 5k

Race Result, Pace: 20:39, 6:40 Pace

Key Notes / Details: (May have been slightly under 5k distance)

Date: October 21st, 2012

Race Name / Distance: Detroit Free Press / International half marathon

Race Result, Pace: 1:39:08, 7:34 Pace

Key Notes / Details:

Based on training and Map my Run distances, I really thought I was capable of a 7:30 half-marathon pace (1:37:30 projected finish), or even slightly faster. Thus, I tried to follow the 7:30 pacer. However, a couple of things became apparent.

1) The pacer seemed to be going faster than I expected. Not much faster – however, there is a difference between a 7:45 mile that I was apparently training at, and a “real” 7:30 mile. This was due to the 3-4% difference between what I thought I was running and the “real” pace.

2) The first 3.5 miles include a decent sized incline on the way up the Ambassador Bridge into Canada, which I had not sufficiently prepared for.

In regard to reason #1, that was another reason to look into a better timing / distance mechanism, which I purchased in early 2013.
Reason #2 – not much I could do! After that race I was more cognizant and tried to work on hill training when I could.

Overall, not a "bad" result, only slightly worse than expected.

Date: November 22nd, 2012

Race Name / Distance: Detroit Turkey Trot / 10k

Race Result, Pace: 43:27, 7:00 Pace

Key Notes / Details:

This was a very congested race, especially as the 10k and 5k finished at the same time in a pretty small area. Folks were at this race in all sorts of costumes (Turkeys and other!). It's not the type of race that you would target a personal best, though I managed to set one (barely!). It's more of an "experience" than a race. There were definitely those of us that were more "serious" about the race, however we were in the minority.

6) 2013 Race Log and Topics

Date	Distance	Time	Personal Best?
4/21/13	Half	1:39:05	
5/5/13	5k	19:32	No, too short, not timed well
5/28/13	5k	20:29	Yes, by 0:10
6/2/13	Half	1:39:09	
7/28/13	8k	34:37	
9/15/13	5k	20:02	Yes, by 0:27
10/20/13	Half	1:36:23	Yes, by 1:00
11/10/13	10k	41:44	Yes, by 1:43

I purchased a Garmin watch in early 2013. In my first run, I immediately realized that many of my standard mapped out routes (e.g. what I thought was a 5k or 4 miler) were measuring about 3-4% shorter than I expected based on estimates and MapMyRun.

Another issue, was that after I started using the Garmin in actual races, I came to realize that many of the US certified races were another 1% longer than Garmin was measuring. When talking to others, I also realized that this was a similar issue observed by other runners relying on Garmin. Everyone's mile "alerts" go off at approximately the same point in the race, and don't seem to line up with mile markers on the course.

This also applied to USATF certified courses that I ran, they seemed slightly longer than expected.

Date: April 21st, 2013

Race Name / Distance: Lansing / Half Marathon

Race Result, Pace: 1:39:09, * 7:30 Pace

Key Notes / Details: First race with a Garmin watch!

* Measured at 13.25 miles

I was hoping for a 1:38 or less, and was pretty much on target the entire race based on my mile splits. One problem though, is that the race doesn't automatically end when you think you've run 13.11 miles. You need to cross the finish line! That didn't happen until about 13.25 miles in based on Garmin! So, the result was as expected (1% too long). It wasn't a big deal to run the last .14 miles, just more of a timing / goal annoyance to me. Other runners seemed to be measuring the distance similar to me, slightly longer than the expected 13.11 miles.

Date: May 5th, 2013

Race Name / Distance: Dash for Destiny / 5k

Race Result, Actual: 19:32, * 6:31 Pace

* Measured at 2.99 Miles

Key Notes / Details: First "badly timed and measured" race.

The race was an early May race, uneventful weather. There were about 150 people running that day. I noticed a couple of major timing issues with the race.

1) I forgot to start my Garmin watch on time, I started it about 10-15 seconds into the race. When I saw the finish line, I noticed that the finish line clock was showing the same time as my watch, which meant that the race clock also started 10-15 seconds after the race started

2) Total distance for the race measured slightly under 3.0 miles, which was low even after adjusting for the 15 seconds.

This gave everyone a big benefit on both time and distance. I knew I wasn't running at a 20:00 pace, and the finish time felt "fake" to me. While I ran the first mile in 6:21, I knew that was too fast, needed to slow down, and actually slowed after the first quarter mile or so. I managed the next 2 miles at a 6:40 pace.

Based on my average 6:34 pace per mile for 2.99 miles, I calculated a **20:25** equivalent 5k pace.

Date: May 28th, 2013

Race Name / Distance: Grand Prix Shakedown, Belle Isle MI / 5k

Race Result, Pace: 20:29, * 6:27 Pace

Key Notes / Details: Lost by one second, nice battle for the line!

* Measured at 3.18 miles

A number of co-workers and I ran a fundraiser on Belle Isle, MI. We participated in this run as part of our ERN (Employee Resource Network), and I did a lot of recruitment to get people to come out after work. There was one relatively younger co-worker (Ryan) who I knew was training pretty well, was in good shape, and had the benefit of being considerably younger than me. I knew he and I would likely finish close to the same time.

Ryan started strong, and was at least 15 seconds ahead after mile 1. My first mile timed in 6:28, and as it was pretty hot, I didn't want to push any further. I decided on the strategy of "let's see if he comes back to the pack". Sure enough, I kept a level pace for mile 2 at 6:34, and could tell I was getting closer to Ryan. Midway through mile three I caught up to him. The difference between 2013 and 2012 (when I passed Mike and Doug), is that I had expended too much effort to catch up on a hot day and couldn't make the strong pass. I also didn't know how long the race actually was (I had a feeling it wasn't exact 5k distance) and couldn't push too early. There was potentially too much of the race left to run. I stayed next to Ryan and hoped I could put in a strong push once I knew we were in sight of the finish line. When the finish line did come into sight, but likely still about a quarter mile away, I increased speed – and to my surprise Ryan was able to match me step for step. I was right behind him though, increased speed a bit more, but he managed to stay ahead. We pretty much stayed that way through the finish. Looking at my pace afterwards, I did the last .18 miles in a 5:45 pace so I was happy with my planning, pacing, and ability to finish strong. Again, I was happy with a strong finish, sometimes you just tip your hat to the other guy. He was obviously tiring over the last two miles, but still picked up his pace and beat me. I finished with an official time of 20:29 compared to Ryan's 20:28. Based on my total measured 6:27 pace per mile for 3.18 miles, I calculated a **20:04** equivalent 5k pace. Pretty close to 20:00 in non-optimum conditions! Sometimes strong competition brings out the best in us.

Date: June 2nd, 2013

Race Name / Distance: Dexter to Ann Arbor run / Half Marathon

Race Result, Pace: 1:39:09, 7:29 Pace

Key Notes / Details: About 3 minutes faster than my time in 2012

Several unofficial successes, and one "Oh, so close"

Date: July 12th, 2013

Race Name / Distance: Practice Run / 5k

Race Result, Pace: 19:59, 6:26 Pace

Key Notes / Details: First "unofficial" 5k under 20:00. I finally did it!

Splits: 6:33, 6:25, 6:26, 5:22 (last .11)

This was a local neighborhood run on my usual 5k practice route. I just decided to push the pace for the first three miles and see where I was at that point. I was approximately 9 seconds over a 20:00 pace after 3 miles, but literally "went all out" over the last 0.11 miles.

It was a **totally awesome feeling** of course, it was a pretty special day for me. I told a few running friends about it (the few that would appreciate it). Other than that, there weren't many others I could share the news with. They wouldn't have a clue as to what I was talking about, or how significant it was!

Date: July 28th, 2013

Race Name / Distance: Electric Bolt / 8k

Race Result, Pace: 34:37, 6:53 Pace

Key Notes / Details: Age group title, beer mug!

Date: September 15th, 2013

Race Name / Distance: Run Wild at the Detroit Zoo / 5k

Race Result, Pace: 20:02, * 6:27 Pace

Key Notes / Details: Closest to a sub 20:00 in an official race!

* Measured at 3.1 miles, so slightly under official 5k distance

I started a bit slow, finished strong, missed it by 2 seconds!

I had not eaten well the day before, and didn't want to push things at the beginning. I didn't think I had a shot at a sub 20:00, but figured I would play it by ear. I was not feeling that great, and felt pretty happy with a 6:39 first mile. I was 13 seconds behind 20:00 pace. My second mile at 6:37 put me 24 seconds behind 20:00 pace. At that point I felt pretty strong and figured I'd give it a shot. I was able to pick up the pace, almost being surprised with my third mile pace of 6:19 bringing me to 17 seconds behind pace. I really put it in gear after mile three, pretty much an all-out sprint to the finish. At the end though, the deficit was too much to make up, but I got **my closest ever** to the official timed 20:00 goal.
6:39, 6:37, 6:17, 5:20 pace for the last .1 mile.

Date: October 1st, 2013

Race Name / Distance: Practice Run / 5k

Race Result, Pace: 19:26, 6:15 Pace

Key Notes / Details: PB by far, optimal conditions

I knew that I didn't have another official 5k lined up for the year, and pretty much went for "all the marbles" on a cool, dry October day. The weather was optimal, I felt good, perhaps started a bit faster than I should have at 6:12 for the first mile, but kept the pace. I had on relatively new shoes, which helped!
My mile splits were 6:12, 6:15, 6:20, with an overall 6:15 pace.

As you continue track your times and set personal bests, you're almost "re-setting the bar" each time. At this point I knew that I could hit the 20:00 mark under decent conditions, it was just a matter of time, and signing up for a 5k sometime in 2014...

Date: October 20th, 2013

Race Name / Distance: Detroit Half Marathon, U.S. portion

Race Result, Pace: 1:36:33, * 7:15 Pace

Key Notes / Details: "Joint" Course

* Measured at 13.3 miles

Detroit US Half Marathon; This was a solid run, but I dealt with cold weather, some unexpected hills, winds in the middle of the course, and a course that was slightly longer than I expected at 13.3 miles.

This race is a relatively new addition to the Detroit marathon weekend race options. You have a choice of running;
- The full marathon
- The first (international) half
- The second half which is run only in the U.S., and for the last 13 miles follows the second half of the full marathon course.

In 2013, the U.S. half started about 2:30 hours after the beginning of the full marathon. While the majority of the faster marathoners already passed through and weren't going to be caught, there were plenty of runners on the course that we would need to pass. For example, a respectable 4:30 marathoner at even splits would be a couple of miles ahead (roughly 15 miles in 2:30), anyone completing the half in say 1:45 would pass them before the race was over.

Thus, there's a lot of weaving around the slower runners that is needed to get through the course. It's an interesting experience but if you are competitive and like to pass people, this can be a lot of fun! As you move through the race, the people you are passing initially (5:00-5:30 marathon finishers) are a lot slower than the ones you will pass later on (4:15-4:30 finishers). Plus, if you're "nice" you can even offer encouragement as you pass others. This weaving around may have added a bit to my time /

distance and may have drained some energy, but I don't think it had a significant impact. I finished one minute ahead of my prior personal best of 1:37:30 set in 2010 (though I still don't understand how I originally ran that time). However, this was 3:00 better than my other half marathons earlier in 2013, and was further proof that continued training and good form was contributing to overall improvement!

Below is a picture of me (on the right) with a friend and fitness coach after we completed the race. We are posing on the side board of a truck with the map course on it, holding our finisher medals!

One of the local well known Detroit running celebrities is Doug Kurtis. Doug has the following "Star Studded" resume:

- He is a 6 time winner of the Detroit marathon, winning it in 1987-1992.
- Doug hold the world record for the most sub 2:20 marathons with 76.
- Doug has won 40 total marathons and has a personal best of 2:13:34.
- In 2013, Doug ran a sub 3:00 marathon (his 200th) at age 61.
- Doug is the Race Director of the Detroit Turkey Trot (20,000+ runners) and Corktown (7,000+ runners) races.
- Doug usually appears at the Detroit marathon expo, and I usually try and say hi when I can. My greeting to him is usually along the lines of "Hi Doug, big fan!".
- Our times are not comparable for those who know the "running math" (Doug is **<u>way faster</u>**, like I said no comparison!)
  - Sub 3:00 marathon at age 61 for Doug
  - 1:36:33 half marathon at age 44 for me
- You can read all about Doug's marathon advice through various publications and news articles, it's quite informative!

Below is a picture of Doug and me (Doug on the left of course) at the 2013 Detroit marathon expo. I had stopped off after work to pick up my race packet, and Doug was nice enough to allow me to take this photo with him. Doug ended up accomplishing his above-mentioned 200th sub 3:00 marathon at age 61, two days after this picture!

Date: November 10th, 2013

Race Name / Distance: Roseville Big Bird 10k

Race Result, Pace: 41:44, 6:40 Pace

Key Notes / Details: 9 MPH for a 10k!

I hadn't been running many 10ks due to trying to hit the 20:00 5k mark. This race was a good 10k to target, as it didn't offer a choice to run a 5k...

I had pretty solid pacing in this one. I do remember it being particularly cold and windy. Again, I started a bit fast but slowed myself down midway through. My 5th and 6th miles involved pretty strong headwinds, so I wasn't surprised with the slightly slower timing. I still felt I had a strong finish, as I passed a few people at the end.

Mile pacing: 6:20, 6:35, 6:45, 6:37, 6:53, 6:48, then a 6:27 pace for the last .26.

Famous Survey: 25 Worst Things to say to a runner (with my responses)

I had seen this survey online and enjoyed reading it from a runner's perspective. I can strongly identify with the questions being asked by non-runners. I figured this is my opportunity to supply my responses as well...

Here goes:

25 worst things to say to a runner

25. Are you fast?
Compared to someone sitting on the couch? Yes.
Compared to other runners in most races? Yes. I'm usually in the top 5-10% of the races I enter, though for some local smaller runs I have finished "on the podium".
Compared to top runners in many races? Not even close. My 5k time of under 20:00 would not get me a college scholarship, but I might make it as an alternate on a high school team. Most college top level athletes are running in the 15:00-16:00 range.
Also, note that even winners of "larger scale" local races would likely not be as competitive on a national or world class scale. For example, one year the winner of the Detroit marathon came in 77th in Boston. I came in 12th in the 2015 Detroit US half marathon, but only 82nd with a similar time in the Dexter Ann Arbor race, as the Ann Arbor race is known for attracting top echelon runners. In 2015, I came in 76th in the Detroit Turkey Trot 10k (39:19), with a time that would be on the podium, if not win, many local races.

24. Wouldn't you rather sleep in?

Sometimes, yes. But

1) Running energizes me, at least for the morning

2) I'm don't like missing training and thinking of the impact on a future race time

3) I have never fallen asleep on a run yet!

23. Don't you get tired?

Sometime a "good" tired, especially with a strong run. I will definitely get sleepy mid-day though if I haven't gotten enough sleep. Nothing that a short 15-20 minute power nap wouldn't solve!

22. You run outside?

Yes, unless I can't. Which means I only have a few short minutes, there is ice on the ground, or it is under 25 degrees and windy.

21. Isn't it too hot?

Almost never! Just keep the hydration commensurate with the weather and take it easy, get used to what your body can do. Whatever you sweat out can (should!) be put back through hydration.

20. Isn't it too cold?

Down to 25 degrees or so (with minimal wind) is fine with me. I prefer cool weather to hot weather, but have a slight issue with keeping my hands warm. I can't seem to find the right gloves that I can use for cold weather runs without getting too hot later in the run! My best approach as of now is to start with light gloves, ball my hands together for the first mile or two, then play it by ear. Other than the gloves though, dress right (layers!) and you're fine.

19. Isn't it too windy?

Only if you're targeting a personal best. It's definitely easier with no wind, and the headwind (especially when cold) can sap your strength. Adjust for it if needed.

18. You run in the rain?

Yes. See #22 above. Though I may pass when it's both cold (under 45 degrees) and rainy. One of my better half marathons was the Dexter Ann Arbor Run in 2015. The weather was relatively cold and rainy for June, and up until the race started I didn't know why I got up early to run. Once it started though, was lots of fun! No worse than a cold shower and you're keeping yourself warm with exercise. Stay out of the big puddles though!

17. Do you really need another pair of running shoes?

Yes. I need to prepare for when these run out. I'm getting close to my 500 mile range and need something in reserve. Besides, they're on sale!

16. Why would you need so many running shoes?

What, so many! There's so much history in each one! They're all different colors! Don't you need at least three extra pairs in case it's raining and or muddy? Don't you need a couple of extra shoes if you need to paint or work in the garden?

15. Running is fun?

Absolutely. Run hard or easy, don't twist an ankle, track yourself on another strong run or recovery session, pass others on the street (believe me, they wish they were in your shoes right now)!

14. Don't you get lost?

Nope. I run on local streets and have a decent sense of direction. However, I'm not too adventurous on my choice of paths. The closest I came to getting lost was when doing a long loop in a city I visited for a work conference, in hot weather, without sufficient hydration. I managed to get through it, but made the mistake of underestimating the length of the run and the need to take along some liquids.

13. Do you need a ride?

Nope. I'm good. There definitely would be some rare cases where a ride would be helpful. Some examples:

- turning an ankle or pulling a hamstring. I don't want to turn an easy 2-3 mile jog back to the starting point into a one hour walk of torture.
- Same if it starts to snow and the ground turns icy.
- Raining and I've already started? No way!
- Other than that, if I'm not "feeling it" I can always take an easy jog back.

One interesting example which will bring out the "essence" of what we do...

Someone driving on a warm day noticed the following: A runner was running on the side of the road, getting in a good sweaty workout, with their face showing obvious effort. The driver rolled down the window and asked "buddy, can I call you a cab? It'll help you get there

sooner!"
Our response is of course "Are you kidding me? The **effort itself** is part of my plan!"

12. What are (those strange exercises) you (are) doing?
Stretching before and after a run? Stride outs? Speeding up and then slowing down (fartleks?) Going all out to finish a (mile / 5k / 10k) based on my time target? Not slowing down and still managing to drink on the run? Squeezing some gelatinous stuff out of a tube into my mouth? Yep, these are things I understand perfectly but don't expect others to have a clue about!

11. Is running safe at your age?
Of course? I'm much healthier than I was before starting to run. In addition to being a healthy habit, it's safer (and cheaper) than lots of other alternatives.

10. Isn't it unhealthy to run so much?
Are you asking that seriously? Too much? I'm only running 3-4 hours a week and fortunately no negative impacts... It might be more unhealthy to spend 3-4 hours a week in front of the TV or bowling and eating pizza...

9. What about your knees?
See notes above. Follow some basic pre and post run stretching, add in some attention to good running form, and hopefully things stay pain free!

8. So your knees do hurt?
They're often a little sore after a long run (long = over 10

miles). No worse than soreness from getting a lot of work done around the house or gardening, playing other sports (i.e. basketball), or biking.

7. How do you hurt yourself running?

Easy ways: turning an ankle, slipping on ice, pulling a hamstring.

Harder but more dangerous: getting hit by a car where the driver is not looking at you, or distracted by something else. My approach is to never assume a vehicle will stop for you until they actually do.

6. What is cross training?

Any non-exercise that's not running. Biking, swimming, weightlifting, Aerobics, elliptical. I don't do a whole lot of that, but I make sure to stretch pretty frequently, and get my "cross training" through long, medium, and slow runs, and incorporating hill training once in a while.

5. How far is your marathon?

A marathon is 26 miles, 385 yards, nothing else is a marathon. My typical race distance is 5k to half marathon. You cannot compare any of the other distances (25k – 15.5 miles or less) to a marathon. Marathons bring a whole new dimension in terms of pre and mid-race fueling, training, and pacing. I tip my hat to regular marathon runners for your determination. To others, don't say you've run one until you've done the full distance (18 mile training runs don't count). Don't say "I could if I wanted", until you've experienced it.

I did run a marathon in April 2015 just to "say I did it". OK – everyone kept on asking me if I ran a marathon so I almost had no choice but to run one! I read lots of material and asked people lots of questions, especially when I kept on bonking in training runs at mile 16!
I ended up running the marathon in 3:23:49 with decent splits (second half "only" six minutes slower than the first half). While it was a great accomplishment, I can definitely say it was one of the hardest things I've done and took a lot of determination to finish at that pace. See Chapter 8 for more details. Perhaps even more details in my next book...

4. But don't you get bored?
Nope. I don't listen to anything while running. I enjoy the scenery, track miles and do mental calculations on my GPS watch, and plan my day.

3. Did you win?
For many of you in training – if you are early on in your running career, even finishing can be considered a small victory, so enjoy every one.
I'm probably one of the few "casual runners" that can actually say I did win a race. (You also don't count as "casual" if you ever were on the track team in school!) I won a few local 5ks with solid sub 20:00 times, usually with participants counts in the 100-200 range. However, the competition in those races is not the same as in some of the bigger ones, and most decent high school (and definitely college) runners easily beat me. Remember, these are athletes that can pretty easily run 5ks in the 17:00-18:00 minute range, with top colleges athletes running 14:00-15:00 (male) and 15:00-16:00 (female).

Regarding “winning”: There is definitely a notion that simply signing up and completing a race for the first time, relatively close to your goal makes you a “winner”. When I completed my first 5k I felt great. When I “finished” my first (and so far only) marathon in the Spring of 2015, I felt fantastic. It was the first time I had run a marathon, and I managed to do pretty well without fading too much at the end.

2. Why do you pay so much to run a race?

I actually don’t pay much to run. The most I paid was a little over $100 to run the Detroit half marathon after missing the early bird special. Most 5k-10ks are in the $25-$40 range, and half marathons $50-$70. For some of the more famous races (Boston, New York, London, etc...) the cost of the race is much higher, without even taking into account airfare, hotel, and miscellaneous expenses.

1. So...you like jogging?

I don’t know, I’ve never done it.

7) 2014 Race Log and Topics

Date	Distance	Time	Personal Best? / other notes
5/4/14	Half	1:36:32	
5/18/14	5k	19:49	First Sub 20:00!
5/26/14	10k	41:36	Yes, by 0:10
6/1/14	Half	1:35:02	
6/8/14	5k	19:13	First Victory!
7/27/14	8k	33:07	
9/14/14	5k	19:34	First combo race
9/14/14	10k	42:01	See above
10/19/14	Half	1:32:20	Yes, by 2:42
11/9/14	10k	39:55	First Sub 40:00!

I ran a lot of "official" events, and had lots of accomplishments!

Date: May 4th, 2014

Race Name / Distance: Novi / Half Marathon

Race Result, Pace: 1:36:32, * 7:20 Pace

Key Notes / Details: Uneven roads, cross traffic, good pacing

* Measured at 13.3 miles

This was a fun half marathon early in the season. It was a relatively strong race, I had pretty even splits through the run. It was a combined race that included a 5k and 10k, so there were actually all sorts of roads where runners were "all over the place", including running in opposite directions in the other lane of a two lane road. Directions, signage, and helpful volunteers made it manageable. Miles 6 to 11 of the half marathon were an out and back that the 5k and 10k runners didn't need to run. I'm sure half marathoners had to withstand the urge to just turn around and go back to the other side and not do the full 3 miles out before turning back! Fortunately when we reached the turnaround, I was happy to see a timing chip at that point making sure folks were honest or at least making everyone else comfortable that the rules were being followed!

Some of the roads were unpaved, and when passing other runners or even running against folks on the other side of the road meant there was less room and you really had to watch your step or risk turning an ankle.

One other story – I had a short conversation with the fellow next to me as I passed him at 6.5 miles, about halfway through the race – I was able to talk easily and he could barely respond. He said he went out "way too fast". I remembered his bib number and checked after the race, he finished in the 1:41 range, or about 5 minutes behind me. This proves the point that on your long runs you should be able to carry on a conversation. That is your indicator that you will have some gas in the tank for the finish! While half marathon race pace is still pretty strenuous for the goal you've chosen, you are not running at 5k / 10k pace and should be able to have a conversation.

5k under 20:00!!!

Date: May 18th, 2014

Race Name / Distance: Groves High School Orchestra / 5k

Race Result, Pace: 19:49, * 6:16 Pace

Key Notes / Details: Duh, first official Sub 20:00!!!! (Also a second place finish overall)

* Measured at 3.16 miles.

While I had already run my personally timed sub 20:00, this was the first "official race" in which I actually ran a full 5k under the 20 minute barrier.

This was an early morning race, it was mostly high school kids running through a subdivision near their school, a couple of miles away from my house. I started in the lead pack of 5-6 people, and one by one the others started to drop off the pace. We probably ran the first quarter mile in 6:00 pace or below, then I realized this wasn't something I could maintain. I dropped the pace to close to 6:15, and maintained throughout.

My mile pacing on GPS was as follows:

Mile Mark	**Speed per mile**
Mile one	6:17
Mile two	6:20
Mile three	6:18
Last .16	0:54 (5:34 pace)
Total (3.16 miles)	19:48 (6:16 pace)

Other notes: I had very consistent splits of 6:17-6:20, and was able to "pick it up" for the last .16

I finished 2nd overall. It was a pretty amazing experience to follow and be in sight of the leader for the entire race. (The winner was a 17 year old kid, so I'm sure I beat him on an "age-adjusted" basis.) I actually gained ground through the race, as he started off in the sub 6:00 pace range and only finished 15 seconds ahead of me.

One thing I noticed during this race and would stress to other runners out there. Somewhere in the first minute, someone in front of me got impatient and just cut right in front of me. It wasn't like he also sped up to avoid collision, he just decided to take advantage of an open lane and didn't care to look behind. He also didn't finish in the top 10 so I'm not sure what his purpose was. Regardless, this can result in a pretty nasty fall as everyone is basically bunched together in the beginning. I was really surprised by it as I hadn't seen something like that before. The third place finisher actually came over to me after the race and commented along the lines of "what was that guy thinking"?

I recommend that you take your time, observe the rules of the road, it's not hard to look around and motion to others if you want to cut in. No one will stop you from trying to switch lanes, especially if you're doing it to speed up or slow down from your current pace, this isn't the Olympics!

Date: May 26th, 2014

Race Name / Distance: Novi Memorial Day / 10k

Race Result, Pace: 41:36, * 6:36 Pace

Key Notes / Details: Don't ease up and let the kid win when you're on a PB pace!

* Measured at 6.3 miles.

Memorial Day 10k. This included a 5k event as well. The 10k started first, about 10 minutes earlier than the 5k. There was some mixing with the slower 5k runners midway through the course, and a common finish. It was

- a small enough race to not worry about parking or restrooms before the race

- I had a good shot at beating my prior 10k PB, but not sure by how much – would depend on how long the course actually was.

Prior PB: 41:44, measured at 6.26 miles.

Result of the current race: 41:07 at 6.22 miles, but 41:36 at the end (6.3 miles). I did get the PB, but only by 8 seconds based on the length of the course.

It was pretty hot and humid that day.

I started a bit too fast as usual, but realized pretty early (first minute in a 6:00 pace) and slowed down my pace. My mile splits were pretty even after that at 6:26, 6:46, 6:41, 6:35, 6:42, 6:36, and about 6:05 pace for the last .3 miles. Long, straight road to the finish so you have the tendency and ability to push a bit more.

One other note: I knew that approaching the finish line I was pretty close to a PB. There was a kid ahead of me, around 10 years old and a "middle of the pack" 5k runner. He was doing well with a (estimated) solid time of a bit over 30 minutes for the 5k. I was steadily gaining ground on him and of course the crowd was cheering mightily for him to beat me. What? Did you think I was going to slow down and let him finish ahead of me? Seriously, I'm on a PB pace here!!!!

(I finished ahead of the kid by 3 seconds, sorry. Next time when I'm not trying to hit a PB I'd probably give up the 3 seconds and make the kid feel good...).

Date: June 1st, 2014

Race Name / Distance: Dexter to Ann Arbor run / Half Marathon

Race Result, Pace: 1:35:09, 7:11 Pace

Key Notes / Details: Nothing major, but continuing to improve vs. the prior year

I finished almost 4 minutes faster than 2013. I finished in 1:35:13 vs my 1:39:08 in 2013. Very comfortable race, I did not feel I was pushing things. My evidence of success again was stable splits, passing people in the last 2-3 miles that were ahead of me through the race, and of course turning it on the last half mile. My overall pace was 7:11, but I ran the 13th mile in 7:03 and the 14th (portion) at a 6:43 pace.

#1!!! First Victory, Favorite Race (and other race concepts)

Date: June 8st, 2014

Race Name / Distance: Stepping Out to Cure Scleroderma / 5K (Detroit Zoo)

Race Result, Pace: 19:13, 6:17 Pace

Key Notes / Details: #1 Finish!!!

Also covers pacing, hills, passing, etc…

The picture below is the starting line of the race.

This is me!
Only my face
and hat are
visible

I'm barely visible, in the dark cap behind the right shoulder of the guy in the light shirt (#122). Dominique (#2 finisher) is slightly ahead of me on my right and behind shirtless Captain America (#223, see next page).

This is of course my <u>favorite race of all time</u>! Seriously, I was able to follow lots of lessons and "known race tips" I've read about, and of course there were a lot of "firsts" for me.

I run in a lot of local races, and will occasionally recognize the usual runners that show up. One very distinct guy in local races, is a guy that dresses up in a Captain America theme. For cold weather it's a full length costume but he uses the "shorts only" look in the summer. He is #223 and in the middle of the front row.

Bib Numbers / Names / Finish

Number	Name	Finish	Where?
73	Joe	19:15 (1)	Behind Tom
313	Dominique	19:51 (2)	Second row, behind #223
122	Tom	20:00	Front
312	Jackie	20:02	Front, #1 female
223	Kevin (Captain America)	20:11	Front
216	John	23:51	Front right
318	Ever	24:56	Front Left
155	Brandon	26:15	Second row
311	Reace (crouching)	27:01	Front Left

The race had about 175 people in it, but despite the relatively small size, actually had a police pace car! (The race was run in Huntington Woods, a relatively well to do neighborhood near the Detroit Zoo).

I started towards the front but not at the front. I crossed the starting line around 1-2 seconds after the start, but in the first group.

Reace, who looked about 11-12 years old shot out of the gate. I didn't think he would be a podium threat, but it was interesting to see his start, and I'm sure it was a thrill for him to start strong. You can see him on the left of the starting line picture.
We started out pretty fast, I was reading under a 6:00 mile pace for the first 30 seconds. I realized that this was not a pace I could maintain, as if someone could maintain a 5:30 - 5:45 pace throughout the race I wouldn't beat him anyway. Better to stay within yourself and keep some strength for the end.

The leader (Dominique) was wearing a singlet (you can see him next to me in the second row in the picture), and was followed by another guy, a guy / girl combo running together, and of course the aforementioned Captain America. I was in 6th place after the first minute. Despite slowing down, we ran the first half mile in 3 minutes (6:00 per mile pace), give or take a few seconds. I slowed down a bit more, right after passing the "couple". At this point I was 4th, and it seemed that Dominique was not putting any more distance between him and the lead group. He still seemed way enough ahead though, I wasn't thinking of larger aspirations at that point.

Slowing down helped, I felt more comfortable and passed the first mile in 6:11. Dominique had an approximate 10 second lead at mile one.

Captain America and the other guy were running together, pretty strong. I slowly closed ground (while again keeping a steady pace) and passed them slightly after mile one. I jokingly said as I passed them "think I can take him?" (referring to Dominique). They responded with something like "go for it, buddy!", which

1) made me feel good about myself – it's always good to get encouragement!

2) provided me with some confidence that they weren't going to be following me in my quest to take over first place.

3) I also felt good that I was still able to talk coherently!

After mile one, I started to reel in Dominique as he started "coming back to me". At somewhere between 1.75 and 2 miles, we were level and both following the police car. Even this part was a first – I had never been a co-leader in a race, certainly not this far in. Along with the excitement, I started to have a nervous feeling and was thinking I'd probably trip or do something else to mess up. At least I didn't need to worry about directions. One good thing about following the police car is that there's little danger of a wrong turn!

I knew there was a medium hill coming up after mile 2. I decided to make a slight move and nudge ahead of Dominique about 30 seconds before the hill. Again, not a major pass, just 2-3 steps ahead at that point. Also, to be honest I wanted to say that I actually **led a race.**

Coming up to the hill, I followed my knowledge and training and actually pulled back on the throttle. I knew not to kill myself by trying to maintain pace on the hill. You're better off conserving energy, using similar effort that you've used until that point, even if you slow down a bit. Sure enough, Dominique put in the extra effort (not sure how he did it, as his pace was obviously dropping) and moved slightly ahead of me at the top of the hill. I did not panic, and did not try to match him, but stated relatively close.

After the hill – I figured that was the time to show strength and I put in a strong pass. I went for it, picked up the pace, and put a good 5 seconds on him. As you can figure based on his initial effort and subsequent effort to pass me on the hill, he could not match me and was left behind.

I couldn't enjoy the last mile though, because it had started to rain and I was afraid to slow down or turn around as I didn't want to screw up and slip. I just kept my pace, followed the police car, waved to the "crowds", and "took it home".

I ended up winning by over 30 seconds. During the race, I was able to target a level, sustainable, pace, along with thinking things through at the heat of the moment. I attributed this to the various books and articles had read – including the fact that a strong pass at the right time can cause the other runner to simply be "looking for second place".

Dominique did hold on for second. The following are my estimates of the race pace:

Mile	Me	Dominique	My Position
1	6:11	6:00	Behind by 0:11
2	6:25	6:35	Tied
Last 1.06	6:37 (or 6:15 pace)	7:13 (6:50 pace)	Ahead by 0:35
3.06	19:13	19:48	Won by 0:35

Overall this was a pretty competitive race. There were 8 people finishing 20:15 or better. I've been in other races where the top 3-4 finish close to 20:00, and the rest of the runners are 3-4 minutes slower.

Below is a pretty grainy picture, but it is actually me crossing the finish line in first place. If you can read it, the time showing on the clock is 29:00, as there was a 10k race that started about 10 minutes before the 5k.

Date: July 27th, 2014

Race Name / Distance: Electric Bolt 8k

Race Result, Pace: 33:07, 6:36 Pace

Key Notes / Details:

This was the same race I had run the year before at 34:37, so about 90 seconds faster (18 seconds per mile). I had a couple of cousins visiting over that weekend, and signed them up to join me. One ran the 5k, one ran the 8k. I'm currently faster than both of them (though they are younger and I'm sure can train harder and catch up to me at some point). It was fun to make this run part of the weekend entertainment!

I had pretty even pacing: 6:27, 6:36, 6:35, 6:53 (uphill portion), 6:28 for the 5th mile, small stretch (sprint) to the finish.

Date: September 14th, 2014

Race Name / Distance: Run Wild Detroit Zoo, 5k (8:00 AM Start)

Race Result, Pace: 19:34, * 6:06 Pace

Key Notes / Details: Masters Champ (in a 1,500 person race). 6:01 3rd mile.

* measured at 3.22 miles

Date: September 14th, 2014

Race Name / Distance: Run Wild Detroit Zoo, 10k (8:45 AM Start)

Race Result, Pace: 42:01, 6:37 Pace

Key Notes / Details: First "combination" (5k / 10k race)

This was a combination 15k, 5k followed by a 10k.

The weather conditions were optimal, cool and dry. There were about 1530 people in the 5k, and another 730 in the 10k. I finished 7th in the 5k, and 9th in the 10k.

A couple of notable facts in this race

- My 5k time of 19:34 was over a distance of 3.22 miles, which turned out slightly faster than my 19:15 victory on June 8th, measured at 3.06 miles.
- I won the 5k masters title, and got to participate in the awards ceremony with a large audience!
- Very solid pacing, at 6:09, 6:14, a pretty amazing 6:01 third mile, and then 1:10 for the last .22 miles (5:30 pace). I'm not sure I can fully explain how I was able to increase my speed to that level for the last mile. I guess I kept on seeing people in front of me that I could pass.

The 10k started 45 minutes after the 5k start, allowing time for folks to go from one race to the other. I actually went back to my car to chill out and drink some Gatorade. When

I got back, the 10k had already started about a minute before so I had some catching up to do.

Other notes from the 10k:

- I ended up running on the shoulder / grass to avoid the large crowd of slower runners at the beginning of the race. I wasn't going to try and weave through that many people! Fortunately the "race officials" didn't disqualify me from running off course. I definitely didn't gain any time / distance, just less people to run through. Other than this race, I usually try to start towards the front in order to avoid the "weave".
- Remember my co-worker Ryan from the 5/28/13 race (he beat me by one second)? He had signed up for the 10k, but not the 5k. We had joked about who had the advantage in the 10k, me because I was already "warmed up" with a 5k, or him because I was tired (of course I was strongly for the latter argument). Due to my late start, Ryan started significantly ahead of me. I ended up passing him halfway through and took it easy at that point – as I started a minute after him I knew he had to beat me by 45-60 seconds in order to have a better net time. As long as he didn't pass me I was OK. I ended up beating him by about 3 minutes, but he did have some sort of excuse such as being up late the night before and playing hockey. I guess we'll need to see what happens in the rubber match!

Date: October 19th, 2014

Race Name / Distance: Detroit Free Press International half marathon

Race Result, Pace: 1:32:20, * 6:58 Pace

Key Notes / Details: I surpassed my prior PB by almost 3 minutes.

* Pace based on 13.24 miles, however I had no way of measuring the actual distance.

A couple of unique things about the race

- This was my first time running the Free Press International half marathon with a Garmin watch. When running through the Detroit Windsor tunnel on the way back in to the U.S., the Garmin loses the signal and stops tracking distance from mile 7 to mile 8. It's quite unnerving for runners like me that are targeting "exact" times. Fortunately, it's only out for a mile and the watch still tracks total elapsed time during the time it loses the satellite. Thus, I was able to do some mental math and figure out my approximate pace. My **actual** Garmin time distance was 12.36 miles, with a roughly 15:00 "eighth" mile due to losing the signal.
- Kevin Sherwood, or Captain America was at the race in full body costume. It was a bit too cold in October for a "shorts only" look! I had pretty even splits, and passed him at mile 5 (pretty hard not to miss his costume). He finished in about one hour, 37 minutes, or 5 minutes behind me.

10k under 40:00!!!

Date: November 9th, 2014

Race Name / Distance: Big Bird 10k

Race Result, Pace: 39:57, *6:20 Pace

Key Notes / Details:

* Measured at 6.3 miles

Another pretty cold day, but it was November…
I was actually targeting sub 40:00 in back of my mind, and knew that would require a 6:25 per mile pace for the entire distance. I needed to allow for some hilly ramps and wind on the second half of the race, including the possibility of an actual race distance greater than 6.22 miles on my GPS. Thus, a 6:15 – 6:20 pace was where I wanted to be.

This race tends to attract high quality runners, and you need to be careful and keep an honest pace or you will be pulled along too quickly. Unfortunately, I got caught up in the pack and despite slowing down after half a mile I ended up at a 6:05 pace through the first mile. I slowed down from that suicidal pace at that point, into a more manageable 6:25 pace for the second mile. About 2 miles in, the eventual women's winner blew past me, If you've ever heard the term "I've been chicked" (passed by a girl ☺) this was the place to use it!
I still felt pretty good about the race. I had slightly positive splits after the initial 6:05 mile, but was able to finish strong and passed a few people (definitely younger than me) right at the end. This was a great feeling as these were people that had run a very solid race at a sub-40:00 10k

pace, but I still had more than they did at the end and was able to pass them.
I'll say it again – It's all about the training and disciplined race pacing!
Mile splits: 6:06, 6:25, 6:28, 6:28, 6:23, 6:20, and a 6:01 pace for the last .3 miles. It's a good thing I picked up the pace to 6:01 for the end, or I wouldn't have gotten the sub 40:00! A 6:15 pace for the last portion instead of 6:01 would have resulted in a 40:00+ finishing time.

Side note: There were folks were calling out split times on the side of the road that were totally inaccurate. For example, if you hear a time and your thought is "there's no way I was going that fast", you probably weren't. Trust yourself, and your own GPS!

8) 2015 Race Log and Topics

Date	Distance	Time	Personal Best? / other notes
4/26/15	Marathon	3:23:49	First Marathon
5/17/15	5k	19:32	
5/31/15	Half	1:33:18	
6/7/15	5k	18:51	Fastest Timed 5k
8/2/15	5k	20:27	Victory #2, but it took 3.3 miles
10/18/15	Half	1:29:45	Yes, by 2:35
11/26/15	10k	39:19	Yes, by 0:36

First (and so far only) Marathon:

Date: April 26th, 2015

Race Name / Distance: Glass City / Marathon

Race Result, Pace: 3:23:49, *7:43 Pace

Key Notes / Details: Marathon! What else needs to be said?

* Measured at 26.44 miles, consistent with Garmin measuring 1% too long

- This run, and the preparation for it would require another 50 pages or so. I'll stay away from it here, but the summary is that:

- I only ran a marathon because I kept on getting the question "So, have you ever run a marathon"?
- I did invest time, training, and read lots of materials about best practices
- While training, I targeted a Boston qualifying pace of 3:25, which was a reasonable target based on my 5K and half-marathon times. I even targeted that time accounting for my Garmin being 1% "over".
- I actually **did** beat my targeted time of 3:25, running 26.44 miles under 3:24:00.
- However, I didn't officially qualify for Boston as in 2016 qualifiers needed to be 2:30 under the target, **I was only 1:11 under my age group target.**
- I continued to have an appreciation for all of the pain and suffering that marathoners go through.
- While I did not achieve negative splits, my drop off wasn't too bad. On my Garmin, I measured
  - 1:37:30 for the first 13 miles (7:30 pace)
  - 1:43:00 for the next 13 miles (7:55 pace)
  - 3:19 for the last .44 miles (7:44 pace)

Date: May 17th, 2015

Race Name / Distance: Groves 5k

Race Result, Pace: 19:32, *6:11 Pace

Key Notes / Details: Improved vs. prior year, but came in 3rd in 2015 vs. 2nd in 2014.

* Measured at 3.16 miles

I improved on my time slightly from the same race I had run 19:44 in 2014. This race was small enough that I was able to check in at the front row of the starting line with last year's winner – "Hey are you Jimmy"? Little did I know that while Jimmy started strong as usual and was a comfortable 15-20 seconds ahead of the pack at .5 miles, there was another runner "Scott" settling into second place biding his time. (I happened to see Scott doing sprint drills in the parking lot prior to the race, and that should have tipped me off.) I was pretty comfortable in third but saw the action unfold in front of me. Scott slowly but surely reeled in Jimmy, and put in a nice pass at about 1.75 miles. I tried to catch up to Jimmy and made up some ground, but couldn't get all the way back at race end. So a good result, decent splits, 12 seconds faster than 2014, and came in 3rd.

Final Standings

Runner	Place	Time
Scott	1	18:52
Jimmy	2	19:21
Joe	3	19:32

Date: May 31st, 2015

Race Name / Distance: Dexter to Ann Arbor run / Half Marathon

Race Result, Pace: 1:33:18, *7:03 Pace

Key Notes / Details: Cool rain? What's the big deal?

* Measured at 13.24 miles

The forecast was pretty cool and rainy, up until now the weather had pretty much been optimal in all of my races. Whenever the forecast predicted rain or snow, it seemed liked it always cleared at race time. This particular morning was pretty cool for late May, the rain started the night before and pretty much continued into the morning. It was the type of race where up until the race started I wasn't sure why I was doing it. People were picking up race packets while huddled against the rain and trying to keep warm and dry. The buses heading to the race start were full of wet people. The race starting line was different than all the years I had seen it. The race starts outside a school building in Dexter, which serves as the staging area. Usually there are crowds all around the building waiting for the start. Today no one was outside, everyone was crammed into the building – while this made the outdoor port-a-potty lines manageable, it didn't help with the humidity levels in the building...

As we got closer to the 8:30 race start, you could see people dragging themselves out into the rain without much enthusiasm – sort of "why are we out here today and not

just back in our warm (and dry) beds”? That was certainly my thought as well.
I was still thinking that as the gun sounded. Even for the 10-15 seconds it took to get to the start timing mat... Strangely enough, all that changed immediately after crossing the starting line. It somehow morphed into “I’m wet anyway, let’s get this baby going” where adrenaline and race excitement just totally took over. No issues whatsoever, and I was able to quickly settle into a steady (cool and wet) race pace. I tried to avoid splashing in deep puddles, but immediately realized that conditions were much more favorable than dry, hot, and humid!

My time improved by about 2 minutes vs. the prior year 2014, but this was due to training as opposed to the cool conditions. My details above regarding the rain were just to illustrate runner “quirks” that seem ridiculous to non-runners. I felt like the race was actually “normal”, and as long I avoided slipping on the roads it wasn’t a big deal.

Date: June 7th, 2015

Race Name / Distance: Scleroderma 5K

Race Result, Pace: 18:51, *6:05 Pace

Key Notes / Details: Fastest timed 5K, despite correcting the timing company and adding 26 seconds!

* Measured at 3.1 miles

This is the same race as my first victory in 2014. While my time was slightly improved, I only came in third place.
Race details:
Two people shot out of the gate, I estimated them at a 5:30 mile pace or so. As I've said before, if they can sustain that, good for them but I'm not going to sacrifice my race to start out with the leaders. Let's see if they come back to the pack. Another girl went out close behind them, but I stayed back.
I could tell that the top two were increasing their distance from me. I pretty much didn't see them for the rest of the race, they finished slightly above 17:00, keeping their 5:30 per mile pace.
The only one I saw coming back to me was the girl. The distance between us shrunk slowly and I passed her at about the two mile mark. She still seemed pretty strong at that point in the race, but she finished in 19:40 and looked like had a hard time recovering at the finish.
Note: Our friend Captain America was there again, he finished 7th in 20:53.

What surprised me most though, was the initial published results showing my finishing time of 18:25. As you participate in more races and get used to your timing device, you'll know when measured results are different than what you expect. Obviously a 5-10 second variance is hard to pick up, but a huge PB when you weren't expecting it is a dead giveaway. This race was one where I know what my Garmin read, and there was a huge discrepancy between Garmin and the initial posted times.

Below is my note to the timing company (after seeing my initial clocking of 18:25)

Dear (Timing Company)
The timing seemed off on yesterday's race, as your published times were faster than how it measured on my watch. Any idea if that was the case (did the clock not start right away)?
I hit a personal best of slightly under 19:00 on my watch, but I am not capable of the 18:25 that shows on the website. I can do one sub 6:00 mile, but not 3 of them!

Response from the timing company:
Joe,
I think I found the issue, there was a ~27 second discrepancy in the time used for start of race.

My Response:
Thanks. Not sure how you can figure that out but much appreciated (especially as it seems right)!

Response from the timing company:

We write down the bib #s of runners at the front of the year start line. I checked those bib numbers in the raw data file and saw the time of the last RFID tag reads for them and got a start time with accuracy of a half second.

My thought:
Not sure what that all meant. Interesting technology, wouldn't you agree?

Victory #2

Date: August 2nd, 2015

Race Name / Distance: End Homelessness 5K

Race Result, Pace: 20:27, *6:13 Pace

Key Notes / Details: A "simpler" win than the first one, but a longer distance than expected

* Measured at 3.29 miles

This was my second overall win. This one was actually more straightforward, less tense than the first one in June 2014. In this race, 6-7 people went out quickly, I let them go and stayed at a 6:00- 6:15 pace for the first minute or two which I knew I could maintain. **Remember, don't try for too fast of a pace (5:30?) if you can't keep it up!** Within the first half mile, I moved into the lead as others dropped their speed. While I did sense footsteps behind me for most of the race and checked to make sure no one was making a run at me, I knew that if others beat me, it would be due to them increasing their pace, rather than me dropping off of my pace. I also knew that there was a good chance that most of the stronger runners would have put in their best effort at the beginning and then tailed off, making it harder for them to pick it up again. I also knew that I had something in reserve at the end if needed. I ended up winning by about 30 seconds.

Sub 1:30 half marathon: Sensing the finish (second best race ever)!

Date: October 18th, 2015

Race Name / Distance: Detroit Free Press U.S. half marathon

Race Result, Pace: 1:29:45, *6:45 Pace

Key Notes / Details: Last half mile in 2:40, sub 1:30 half marathon!

* Measured at 13.3 miles

You can read my description of the course from the section describing the 10/20/13 race. My 2013 time was 1:36:23, so I ran it almost 7 minutes faster (30 seconds per mile) in 2015. The start was also slightly different than 2013, as we started 3 hours after the marathon start instead of the 2.5 hours in 2013.

Based on my prior running of this course in 2013, I knew that it would measure longer than 13.1 on my GPS. Going in, I knew I had an outside shot at a sub one hour and 30 minutes, but I needed to adjust for the course length. I added some conservatism, and targeted to finish **13.3** miles in 1:30, or a 6:45 pace. My first 6 miles were almost "easy" and I was on pace. However, I was then hit by pretty strong winds and an "over and back" on a bridge during miles 7-10. By the time I saw my 7:03 clocking for the tenth mile, I knew I was in trouble. I actually swallowed an extra gel at mile 10 for energy, which was a gamble as I hadn't been training using the extra gel. Perhaps it gave me some physiological lift? Despite the absence of wind, miles 11 and 12 weren't much better at 6:50 and 6:54. Right after a big incline to finish mile 12 and beginning mile 13, I felt like I was running out of energy. I went from being 28 seconds under pace through mile 7, to at least 10-15 seconds over pace after mile 12. I wasn't keeping an exact count, but knew that my chances of hitting the 1:30 goal were pretty slim. I decided to do something a bit drastic as I didn't think I could maintain a solid pace for the next 8-9 minutes it would take me to finish. **I actually slowed down and walked for 10 seconds.**

At that point, there was perhaps another motivating factor. I had something happen that doesn't usually happen to me towards the end of a race (due to my disciplined pacing of course ☺) in that another runner actually caught up to me and was threatening to pass me by! Even worse, it looked like an "older" guy in **my** age group!
However, I knew the finish line was coming….
I got back to my 6:45 pace after my brief walk at the end of mile 12, but that wasn't going to be enough. Somehow as I got within a half mile of the finish, desperation set in and I "picked it up" without noticing how fast I was actually going, and for how long.

As you see on the Garmin read below showing the various stages of the race; I was at a 6:40-6:45 pace most of the race until the last half mile when my pace increased considerably.

Full race: 1:29:45

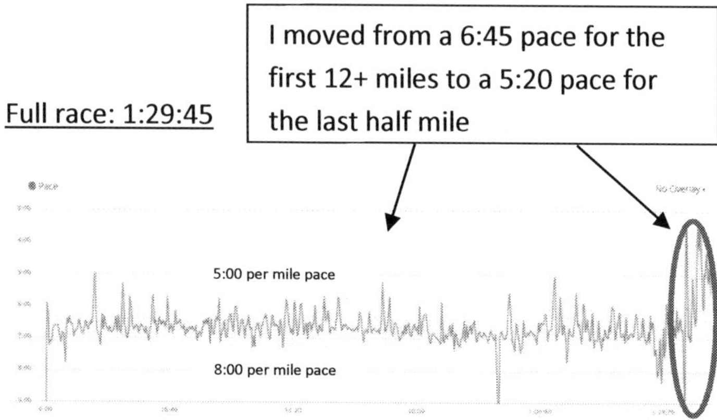

Last 15 minutes

Last 6 minutes

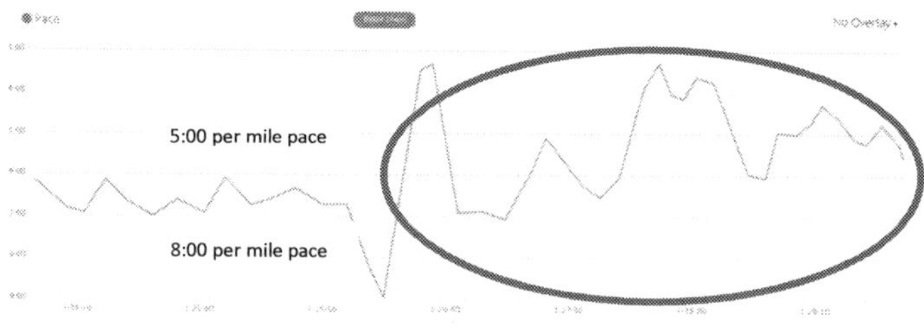

It looks like **my last half mile was at a 5:20 pace**, or roughly 2:40 for 800 meters. My "real" mile splits on Garmin confirmed my estimates, showing the last segment of .31 miles run in 1:39, or at a 5:15 pace.

Doing the math, my last half mile saved me 40-45 seconds from my actual pace through 12.8 miles (dropping from 3:20-3:25 per half mile to 2:40 for the last half mile) and put me over the top to finish 15 seconds under my target. Here's the pure mile splits as per GPS:

		Gap (Seconds) vs. Target (6:46)	
Mile	Mile Speed	Per Mile	Cumulative
1	6:46	0	0
2	6:42	-4	-4
3	6:40	-6	-10
4	6:42	-4	-14
5	6:40	-6	-20
6	6:39	-7	-27
7	6:45	-1	-28
8	6:47	+1	-27
9	6:54	+8	-19
10	7:03	+17	-2
11	6:50	+4	+2
12	6:54	+8	+10
.8	7:00 (est.)	+14	+24
.5	2:40 (5:20 pace)	-40 (2:40 vs. 3:20 for a half mile)	-14 (rough calc)
13.3	1:29:45	-15	Final time

Below is a picture of me close to the finish in that race. You can see the concentration, but looking at this I don't seem to be overly exerting myself. Feel free to look up my bib number and result!

Interestingly enough, I've **never** run 800 meters (half a mile) that fast. My previous best for 800 meters was in the 2:45+ range, of course without running 13 miles first!

I guess desperation, sight of the finish, and pure stubbornness gave me an extra boost. The crowd was great as well, remember there was a lot of cheering as this is the joint half marathon and marathon finish. (It was about 4:30 hours after the official marathon start time, so there were still lots of runners completing the marathon.)

Another side note from the race: For the first 6-7 miles, I was running relatively close to a guy wearing various Ironman 70.3 gear. For those that are not familiar with the terminology, Ironman 70.3 is a half Ironman where participants complete a 1.2 mile swim, followed by a 56 mile bike ride, and then a half marathon run of 13.1 miles. I knew this guy must be in pretty decent shape but I was staying pretty even with him. About 7 miles in, while battling the strong headwinds he caught up, passed me, and remarked on his way by "Wow, it took me 7 miles to get warmed up". Pretty disheartening for me to say the least. However, I knew my limitations and did not try to push it at the time. It may have been a ploy, he may not have been feeling great then either but it wasn't worth it to try and match him at that point in the race. I watched him slowly but surely put distance between us, and didn't think much more until the race end. When I got to the finish line, I saw him there, looking like he had not finished much before me. It turned out he finished about 15 seconds ahead of me, and was 11th overall, third overall male masters finisher. I was one place behind and thus slightly out of the prize money category (small cash prize for top 3 overall and top 3 masters).

My work colleague Paul (quoted on the back cover of this book) is a two time full Ironman finisher. I get a lot of inspiration from the dedication and training he puts in to compete at the three Ironman disciplines.

Date: November 26th, 2015

Race Name / Distance: Detroit Turkey Trot 10k

Race Result, Pace: 39:15, *6:14 Pace

Key Notes / Details: PB 10k, outstanding weather conditions. 76th out of 6000+ participants

* Measured at 6.28 miles

Another personal best, under cool but optimal conditions. A strong race, with pretty even pacing. As usual, I felt good about keeping a disciplined pace, and being able to pass people towards the end who were fading from an early fast pace.

I had kept up with my training, and was able to do something I never would have believed possible 2 years before. A sub 6:15 pace for 10k? As my seven year old son would say, "Seriously"?

On the next page is a picture of me running at a recent Turkey Trot event in downtown Detroit. It's close to the 5 mile mark of the 10k race.

9) Other Random Topics

Gear, Hydration, GPS, Run vs. other exercise, Support crew

A) Gear:

Running clothing, hat, socks, shoes etc...
My general approach is to try and keep away from cotton as much as possible. This goes from running shorts, to shirts, and socks. Use lightweight, synthetic materials, and use layers if it's cold.

As far as gloves for cold weather (noted earlier), I still can't say I've found the perfect solution. You need something pretty warm for when you first start, but after running for 10-15 minutes you will usually warm up enough to either
- take the gloves off (if it's 35 degrees or more)
- switch to lightweight gloves (if it's a bit colder).

So far, my best solution has been relatively inexpensive lightweight (but soft) garden gloves, and to "ball your hands together" for the first ten or fifteen minutes.

B) Hydration System:

I purchased a hydration belt with clip on sports bottles. This was one of the best purchases I have made. In my mind, a couple of hydration bottles that you can easily carry with you, and don't get into the way of running, are essential. You never know exactly how far you are running, how hot and humid it is outside, how you are feeling, where you will end up, and what type of detour you may want to follow. (hey, let's do one more loop / check out that foliage!)

For the 10-20 elite professionals running in planned events – no need to do this. You have stations set up with your beverage of choice. For others in well-organized events, have good discipline, and are OK with drinking whatever you get at the well-spaced fluid stations, no need.

For everyone else, or for training runs...
Get a hydration system! I highly recommend it.

Two question to keep in mind when making your decision
1) Do I need to think about it when I'm running – the answer should be "NO"!

This is why I stay away from anything handheld, as I don't want to think about it during the run. It would definitely impact my stride (especially if I need more than one bottle). Also, if you're wearing a waist pack, it needs to be loose enough to allow circulation, but tight enough to not bounce or make your clothes shift!

2) Is it easy to access when I need it – answer should be "YES"!

The right hydration system (and each person will have their own preference) is like a security blanket during a race and eliminates one more item of worry. You can easily get at it without stopping or slowing down.
It removes the worry of making sure you can find a drink (and the right drink) somewhere. You know exactly what you are drinking and more important, how much! You can drink when you need to, not just when you pass a water station. How many of you have either

- passed on a drink and regretted it later
- drank when you didn't need to because you didn't want to "take a chance" of missing another fluid station?

C) GPS / Timing Watch:

Get a GPS enabled watch or other "distance tracking stuff". You may ask, why bother? I can always estimate as I've measured this route and know exactly how long it is! Or, I run on XYZ trail and the miles are clearly marked, what more do I need? Also, why can't I just take my phone with me and use an app to track my progress?

Answer:
Last point first: I don't carry a phone with me, it's too bulky. It's also a pain in the neck to pull it out and "unlock". Other points raised: All good points, and ones that I used for my first 4 years of running. However, I can say that without question a real GPS is very important if you're serious about your times and races. I have found it crucial for mid-race (or mid-run) pacing. You will benefit from knowing your pace during the run and between markers, as well as being able to analyze your runs after the fact. You can look at your pacing on hills vs. flat surfaces, and not panic due to incorrect distance markers on the road. You can also go in all sorts of directions and be able to track your distance accurately. Basically, be in much more control, and minimize the uncertainty.

D) Running vs. other exercise:

For the amount of time invested, compared to other sports running will

- burn more calories
- require less preparation
- is much cheaper
- is much more common to discuss in a social setting
- doesn't necessarily require getting a group together (unlike pickup basketball), unless of course you need the motivation
- doesn't require a specific skill set or coordination. Just need to move those feet!

E) Support Crew:

The two people you most need to support you in your running habit are;

1) Your spouse (and kids): Someone needs to understand why you need to disappear a couple of times a week and not be accessible. Also, if applicable they need to watch the kids (and be OK with it) whenever you aren't there! Of course, you need to reciprocate when they need to get out as well...

Don't worry, you'll feel appreciative, somewhat guilty (it will be hard to claim laziness), and your running will also give you additional energy to help around the house. You can always use another trip up and down the stairs to Cross Train and build leg strength! Talk to the kids, share the math and running stories. Now, when I come back from a local race the typical question they ask is "Did you win"?

2) Your boss. He (or she) is a great person to talk to. You

won't want to hide this habit - especially if you need to get out for a quick lunch run or be slightly late for a meeting in the morning. Regarding missing work, running isn't much worse of an excuse than family (OK, this might be a bit of a stretch), and your boss should be supportive. Some bosses can actually be pretty good motivators, as I would definitely point to a conversation I had with my boss sometime in 2006-2007 as one of the drivers of my running habit. "Dave" had been considering the track team in college but eventually joined the wrestling team. This gave him some running background and we were able to "talk shop".

Dave talked to me about his own goal. It was targeting, and then running, a 6 minute mile after he had turned 50. He was a lot heavier than me, and I thought "wow, that's impressive. If he can do that, there's no reason I can't do the same." That was actually one of my motivating factors to start my running "career". Since then, while I haven't always reported directly to him I've kept in touch, and we've shared running (and other exercise) progress and tips over the years.

Annoying habits of Runners

Here is a list of (some of) the annoying and weird things that runners do.

1) We talk about running. (Almost) all the time.
2) We talk about how great & fun running is, and make people feel guilty for not running.
3) We bring our running shoes on vacation.
4) We generate a steady flow of wet, sweaty clothes.
5) We pick the dead skin off our feet and clip (dead) toenails.
6) We say things like, "I have to get home; I've got a long run in the morning."
7) Or, "I'm not drinking; I've got a long run in the morning."
8) Or, "Oh, it was hot / cold / rainy? I ran this morning"
9) Or, of course, adding any phrase in front of "I've got a long run in the morning" just to let you know that we have a long run in the morning.
10) We share details of our running events with others.
11) We do all sorts of stretching exercises without caring who is watching.
12) We know what the following (and other) running terms mean: Heel strike, foam roller, fartleks, bib, "chicked", chip & gun time.
13) We say things like "I did an easy 8 miler." 8 miles is never easy, but that doesn't mean it isn't fun. Also, we do know there's a clear difference between
"I did an easy 8 miler" and
"I pushed the pace on a 8 miler today"

14) We think way too much about sock purchases, with very little consideration as to whether they actually match.

15) We wear weird things like compression sleeves and hydration belts while we run.

16) We set our alarm clocks, keep on hitting snooze, but eventually get out of bed. To our spouses / roommates: sorry!

And last but not least...

17) We assume that everyone is as passionate about running as we are.

This is by no means a complete list of our annoying habits. Feel free to add more in the space below!

10) Conclusion:

I've obviously had lots of fun, both with running, tracking, and documenting my progress. I've met and made new friends, and stayed relatively injury free.

There a limit to how much additional improvement I can make to my running times, so I may just get slightly better as I get older, or even just hope to maintain my current fitness and speed.

Thus ends my journey, or perhaps it's only the beginning...

<u>Quotes:</u>
"Having a goal, executing a plan and consistency are the key elements to success. I have known Joe for some time and he embodies the athlete spirit, having the discipline to overcome the rigors of a challenging training program."
Kevin Cohen, NAASFP-MC.

"Joe has taken running to a level of performance and training efficiency that I highly admire! The lessons and experiences in this book show how you can get there as well. Joe breaks it all down and takes the mystery out of getting faster."
Paul Mozak, colleague and 2X Ironman finisher.

11) Appendix: Running Logs 2012-2015

2012 Running / Race Log (Page 1)

	(Miles)		Pace		
Date	**Distance**	**Time**	**Min / Mile**	**MPH**	**Notes**
1-Jan	5	36:28	7:18	8.23	
8-Jan	5	36:02	7:12	8.33	
15-Jan	5.71	44:02	7:42	7.79	Indoor track
22-Jan	5	37:53	7:35	7.92	Indoor track
26-Jan	3.76	27:22	7:17	8.24	
29-Jan	5	37:03	7:25	8.10	
1-Feb	2	13:38	6:49	8.80	
2-Feb	12.15	1:37:20	8:01	7.49	
5-Feb	2	14:12	7:06	8.45	
9-Feb	5	36:56	7:23	8.12	
12-Feb	4	28:42	7:11	8.36	Indoor track
15-Feb	7.26	55:15	7:37	7.88	New hydration bottles / belt
17-Feb	4	28:24	7:06	8.45	
19-Feb	5.06	37:42	7:27	8.05	
21-Feb	3.14	21:42	6:55	8.68	
23-Feb	8.87	1:06:55	7:33	7.95	
26-Feb	4	28:24	7:06	8.45	
1-Mar	10.01	1:17:04	7:42	7.79	
4-Mar	4.17	29:58	7:11	8.35	
6-Mar	7.18	54:17	7:34	7.94	
9-Mar	3.2	23:18	7:17	8.24	
11-Mar	4	28:51	7:13	8.32	
13-Mar	4.2	30:51	7:21	8.17	
15-Mar	10.82	1:24:25	7:48	7.69	
18-Mar	4.95	36:30	7:22	8.14	
20-Mar	4	27:57	6:59	8.59	Tried "new form" running
22-Mar	4.95	35:57	7:16	8.26	
23-Mar	3.14	21:28	6:50	8.78	
25-Mar	5.34	40:06	7:31	7.99	
29-Mar	11.61	1:29:00	7:40	7.83	
1-Apr	4	27:14	6:49	8.81	
3-Apr	4.36	31:14	7:10	8.38	
5-Apr	8.25	57:57	7:01	8.54	loop around the zoo
9-Apr	3.14	22:29	7:10	8.38	
11-Apr	10.14	1:16:17	7:31	7.98	
16-Apr	3.14	21:22	6:48	8.82	
18-Apr	6.26	47:52	7:39	7.85	
22-Apr	13.1	1:44:15	7:57	7.54	Lansing half marathon
25-Apr	4	28:40	7:10	8.37	
27-Apr	5	35:40	7:08	8.41	
29-Apr	4	30:10	7:33	7.96	
30-Apr	6.2	46:20	7:28	8.03	Estimated distance, no drinks
3-May	8.25	1:01:30	7:27	8.05	
9-May	4	28:01	7:00	8.57	
11-May	4.44	30:53	6:57	8.63	
13-May	4	29:15	7:19	8.21	Hill training
15-May	4	27:40	6:55	8.67	
17-May	13.14	1:41:45	7:45	7.75	Long run before Dexter neg. splits
20-May	4	29:10	7:18	8.23	
22-May	4.32	29:42	6:52	8.73	

Note: 2012 distances are estimated / MapMyRun, and times are likely 3-4% too fast

2012 Running / Race Log (Page 2)

	(Miles)		Pace		
Date	Distance	Time	Min / Mile	MPH	Notes
24-May	8.25	1:00:58	7:23	8.12	
25-May	2	13:33	6:47	8.86	
29-May	3.1	21:38	6:59	8.60	Grand Prix Shakedown, 85 degrees
31-May	4	30:27	7:37	7.88	
3-Jun	13.1	1:42:22	7:49	7.68	Dexter Ann Arbor run
6-Jun	4				7 Intervals (1:28, 1:29), 6:16 mile
8-Jun	4	26:47	6:42	8.96	
10-Jun	5.26	37:28	7:07	8.42	
12-Jun	3.5				10 Intervals (1:24, 1:25), + one mile
14-Jun	8.25	57:57	7:01	8.54	
15-Jun	2.5				Intervals, 1.22 - 1:24, 6:08 mile
17-Jun	3.25				Intervals, 9 400s, with 2 at 1:20
19-Jun	3.14	20:30	6:32	9.19	
21-Jun	3				Intervals, 8 400s, 1 at 1:19
22-Jun	2				
24-Jun	3.1	21:12	6:50	8.77	Scleroderma 5k, #1 masters
26-Jun	3				Intervals, 7 400s, 800 in 3:07, 1:24
28-Jun	13.14	1:39:13	7:33	7.95	
1-Jul	3				Intervals, 1:21 400, 3:01 800
4-Jul	4.62	32:48	7:06	8.45	
6-Jul	2.25				
11-Jul	2.5	17:00	6:48	8.82	
13-Jul	2.9	21:00	7:14	8.29	
15-Jul	3.45				Intervals
17-Jul	3.14	21:04	6:43	8.94	
19-Jul	11.48	1:29:13	7:46	7.72	
20-Jul	1.5				Short run, include 1 mile at 6:35
22-Jul	5.5	39:00	16:11	3.71	
24-Jul	4.5				Intervals, half 1:23, 3:02
26-Jul	4.25				Intervals (1:25), half, mile (6:40)
27-Jul	2	13:05	6:33	9.17	
30-Jul	4	27:25	6:51	8.75	
1-Aug	4.25				Intervals, 800 at 2:57
3-Aug	9.89	1:15:27	7:38	7.86	
5-Aug	6	44:33	7:26	8.08	
7-Aug	4.25				Intervals, 400s and a few 800s (3:02)
10-Aug	2	13:18	6:39	9.02	
12-Aug	3.1	20:39	6:40	9.01	Milford 5k
14-Aug	4				Intervals (1 1:21), easy mile (6:29)
15-Aug	5.16	35:42	6:55	8.67	
22-Aug	4.25				Intervals, 400s (1:25), 800s (2:58)
24-Aug	9.74	1:12:50	7:29	8.02	
26-Aug	3.5				Intervals, 6 400s, 1.25, half (3:12)
28-Aug	3	21:30	7:10	8.37	
30-Aug	10.1	1:15:11	7:27	8.06	
2-Sep	4.5				100s, 200s, 400s (1:19), 800
4-Sep	3.14	20:45	6:36	9.08	
6-Sep	8	56:29	7:04	8.50	
9-Sep	5				Intervals
11-Sep	4	27:10	6:48	8.83	

Note: 2012 distances are estimated / MapMyRun, and times are likely 3-4% too fast

2012 Running / Race Log (Page 3)

	(Miles)		Pace		
Date	**Distance**	**Time**	**Min / Mile**	**MPH**	**Notes**
13-Sep	13.13	1:37:50	7:27	8.05	Long(er) run training
16-Sep	4	26:43	6:41	8.98	
20-Sep	3.14	21:32	6:51	8.75	Practice 5k
21-Sep	8.5	1:02:41	7:22	8.14	
23-Sep	4.25				Intervals, with a 2:55 800
25-Sep	4	28:07	7:02	8.54	
28-Sep	8.74	1:03:26	7:15	8.27	
30-Sep	4.25				Intervals, with a 1:20 quarter
3-Oct	4	28:24	7:06	8.45	
5-Oct	5	34:42	6:56	8.65	
7-Oct	8.00	57:43	7:13	8.32	
11-Oct	11.62	1:27:03	7:29	8.01	
16-Oct	6	41:53	6:59	8.60	
18-Oct	4	29:08	7:17	8.24	Easy, 3 days before Detroit
21-Oct	13.1	1:39:08	7:34	7.93	Free press half marathon
24-Oct	5	34:06	6:49	8.80	
26-Oct	3.17	20:48	6:34	9.14	
28-Oct	5.16	35:41	6:55	8.68	
1-Nov	6.08	42:34	7:00	8.57	
4-Nov	3				Intervals, 400 at 1:20
4-Nov	2.42	16:31	6:50	8.79	
6-Nov	4.2	28:35	6:48	8.82	First 3.14 in 21:07, rest "easy"
8-Nov	10.12	1:11:05	7:01	8.54	
11-Nov	6.25	42:01	6:43	8.93	
13-Nov	4	26:36	6:39	9.02	
14-Nov	4.12	28:29	6:55	8.68	
18-Nov	5.12	36:15	7:05	8.47	Estimated
22-Nov	6.21	43:27	6:60	8.58	Turkey Trot Detroit, 10k PB
23-Nov	3.26	22:37	6:56	8.65	
25-Nov	5	33:49	6:46	8.87	
27-Nov	4	27:02	6:46	8.88	
29-Nov	4.53	31:02	6:51	8.76	
2-Dec	8.07	57:00	7:04	8.49	
4-Dec	4.9	34:55	7:08	8.42	
7-Dec	3.66	24:38	6:44	8.91	
9-Dec	7.07	48:32	6:52	8.74	
11-Dec	1				
13-Dec	7.49	51:49	6:55	8.67	
16-Dec	3				
18-Dec	3.14	21:00	6:41	8.97	
20-Dec	6.16	42:56	6:58	8.61	
24-Dec	4.27	30:07	7:03	8.51	
25-Dec	15	1:54:02	7:36	7.89	Longest run (at the time)
30-Dec	5	34:32	6:54	8.69	Indoor track - estimate

Note: 2012 distances are estimated / MapMyRun, and times are likely 3-4% too fast

2013 Running / Race Log (Page 1)

Date	(Miles) Distance	Time	Pace Min / Mile	MPH	Notes
1-Jan	4.6	31:51	6:55	8.67	
4-Jan	2.48	18:08	7:19	8.21	Icy, plus too many cars out!
6-Jan	5.12	35:00	6:50	8.78	
9-Jan	3.56	30:29	8:34	7.01	
10-Jan	4	28:06	7:02	8.54	
13-Jan	7.18	51:14	7:08	8.41	
16-Jan	5	34:38	6:56	8.66	
18-Jan	3.14	20:57	6:40	8.99	
20-Jan	5	35:14	7:03	8.51	Indoor track
24-Jan	2.14	18:57	8:51	6.78	11 degrees - way too cold!
27-Jan	5.1	35:37	6:59	8.59	
29-Jan	6	47:22	7:54	7.60	
31-Jan	3				Indoor track
3-Feb	5	36:02	7:12	8.33	
5-Feb	4.5				Indoor track
7-Feb	5.01	34:59	6:59	8.59	First run with Garmin!
10-Feb	6.21	43:51	7:04	8.50	practice 10k
12-Feb	4.01	27:48	6:56	8.65	
14-Feb	10.16	1:15:21	7:25	8.09	
17-Feb	2.78	20:09	7:15	8.28	
19-Feb	5.01	35:45	7:08	8.41	
20-Feb	4.5				Indoor track
25-Feb	4	28:38	7:09	8.38	
26-Feb	5.01	36:41	7:19	8.19	
4-Mar	4.01	27:44	6:55	8.68	
6-Mar	2	12:33	6:17	9.56	
7-Mar	11.03	1:23:29	7:34	7.93	Longer training run
10-Mar	5.3	37:09	7:01	8.56	
12-Mar	3.15	20:55	6:38	9.04	
14-Mar	8	58:51	7:21	8.16	
17-Mar	5.5	39:09	7:07	8.43	24 degrees
21-Mar	12.14	1:34:00	7:45	7.75	Hydration bottles froze!
24-Mar	3.11	20:22	6:33	9.16	Solid 5k
28-Mar	5.02	34:35	6:53	8.71	
31-Mar	4.5				Intervals
4-Apr	13.11	1:40:00	7:38	7.87	Half marathon training
7-Apr	7.01	49:49	7:06	8.44	
8-Apr	1	7:30	7:30	8.00	
12-Apr	6.75	47:54	7:06	8.46	
14-Apr	9	1:06:13	7:21	8.16	
16-Apr	4	26:56	6:44	8.91	
18-Apr	5.01	36:43	7:20	8.19	Easy 5 prior to Lansing
21-Apr	13.25	1:39:05	7:29	8.02	Lansing Half Marathon
23-Apr	3.11	21:11	6:49	8.81	
25-Apr	10.01	1:14:40	7:28	8.04	
28-Apr	5				Intervals
30-Apr	8.01	58:44	7:20	8.18	
2-May	13.11	1:40:57	7:42	7.79	
5-May	2.99	19:32	6:32	9.18	Dash for Destiny 5k

2013 Running / Race Log (Page 2)

Date	(Miles) Distance	Time	Pace Min / Mile	MPH	Notes
5-May	1.5				
7-May	6.21	42:30	6:51	8.77	PB 10k at the time
8-May	3.11	21:33	6:56	8.66	
10-May	3.11	20:33	6:36	9.08	
12-May	12.5	1:36:26	7:43	7.78	Long run, some hills
14-May	5.5	38:39	7:02	8.54	
17-May	5.01	34:23	6:52	8.74	
19-May	8.09	59:59	7:25	8.09	Hills, prep for Dexter
21-May	3.5				Intervals
23-May	13.11	1:37:13	7:25	8.09	Solid Half
26-May	6.21	45:14	7:17	8.24	
28-May	3.18	20:29	6:26	9.31	Grand Prix Shakedown 5k
30-May	5.09	37:55	7:27	8.05	Prep prior to Dexter
2-Jun	13.24	1:39:09	7:29	8.01	Dexter Half marathon
4-Jun	3.81	27:28	7:13	8.32	
6-Jun	9.01	1:04:28	7:09	8.39	
9-Jun	4	27:12	6:48	8.82	
11-Jun	2.5	20:00	8:00	7.50	Estimated
13-Jun	10.01	1:13:58	7:23	8.12	
16-Jun	6.61	47:06	7:08	8.42	
18-Jun	5.01	42:34	8:30	7.06	Intervals
20-Jun	13.51	1:39:29	7:22	8.15	Half in sub 1:36:30, PB
23-Jun	5.5	41:02	7:28	8.04	
26-Jun	3.5	24:41	7:03	8.51	
27-Jun	9.33	1:09:44	7:28	8.03	
30-Jun	7.01	50:10	7:09	8.38	
2-Jul	4.01	26:57	6:43	8.93	
4-Jul	4.13	29:19	7:06	8.45	With daughter on rollerblades
5-Jul	4.11	29:00	7:03	8.50	
7-Jul	6.21	43:10	6:57	8.63	
10-Jul	12.01	1:31:56	7:39	7.84	
12-Jul	3.11	19:59	6:26	**9.34**	First time sub 20:00!!!
12-Jul	2.01	15:39	7:47	7.71	Cool down run
14-Jul	6.5	47:24	7:18	8.23	
17-Jul	4.54	31:26	6:55	8.67	
22-Jul	2	13:30	6:45	8.89	
23-Jul	4.03	29:28	7:19	8.21	
25-Jul	13.11	1:38:25	7:30	7.99	
28-Jul	5.03	34:37	6:53	8.72	Electric Bolt 8K
30-Jul	4.5	38:54	8:39	6.94	Intervals
1-Aug	9.5	1:09:12	7:17	8.24	
4-Aug	3.75	26:59	7:12	8.34	
6-Aug	4	26:34	6:39	9.03	First 5k in 20:12
8-Aug	9.01	1:09:56	7:46	7.73	
11-Aug	5.11	37:50	7:24	8.10	
13-Aug	4.01	30:35	7:38	7.87	Fartleks
15-Aug	8.01	57:55	7:14	8.30	
18-Aug	4.3	31:33	7:20	8.18	
20-Aug	3.11	21:55	7:03	8.51	
23-Aug	13.11	1:38:50	7:32	7.96	Pratice Half

2013 Running / Race Log (Page 3)

	(Miles)		Pace		
Date	**Distance**	**Time**	**Min / Mile**	**MPH**	**Notes**
25-Aug	7.05	51:27	7:18	8.22	
27-Aug	4.01	27:01	6:44	8.91	
29-Aug	7.75	58:38	7:34	7.93	Hill training
2-Sep	18.01	2:26:56	8:10	7.35	Long run training
4-Sep	1.63	12:00	7:22	8.15	
9-Sep	3.5	24:17	6:56	8.65	
10-Sep	5.01	34:48	6:57	8.64	
12-Sep	12	1:28:03	7:20	8.18	
15-Sep	3.1	20:02	6:28	9.28	Run Wild 5k - missed by :02!
15-Sep	1.25	8:41	6:57	8.64	
17-Sep	8.64	1:00:01	6:57	**8.64**	1 hour PB at the time
22-Sep	6	47:28	7:55	7.58	Intervals
24-Sep	10.5	1:14:58	7:08	**8.40**	10 Mile PB at the time (1:11:35)
29-Sep	8.13	57:43	7:06	8.45	
1-Oct	3.11	**19:26**	6:15	**9.60**	Personal best 5K (at the rime)!!
1-Oct	0.89	6:48	7:38	7.85	
3-Oct	13.11	1:35:00	7:15	8.28	half training
7-Oct	2.01	12:58	6:27	9.30	
9-Oct	5.26	36:18	6:54	8.69	
11-Oct	11	1:19:47	7:15	8.27	
13-Oct	8.01	57:38	7:12	8.34	
15-Oct	3.11	19:44	6:21	9.46	Training 5k
15-Oct	1	7:15	7:15	8.28	
17-Oct	6.56	47:00	7:10	8.37	
20-Oct	13.31	1:36:23	7:14	8.29	Detroit US Half marathon
22-Oct	5.01	35:34	7:06	8.45	
27-Oct	6.22	41:44	6:43	**8.94**	PB 10k at the time
31-Oct	7.01	50:24	7:11	8.35	
3-Nov	1.01	9:09	9:04	6.62	
3-Nov	0.51	2:58	5:49	10.31	
3-Nov	2.65	19:23	7:19	8.20	
5-Nov	4.5	35:45	7:57	7.55	Intervals
7-Nov	12.11	1:28:13	7:17	8.24	
10-Nov	6.26	41:44	6:40	**9.00**	Big Bird 10k
12-Nov	3.13	21:42	6:56	8.65	
15-Nov	9.01	1:02:58	6:59	**8.59**	Solid 9 miles
17-Nov	7.2	50:07	6:58	8.62	Fartleks
19-Nov	4	26:07	6:32	9.19	
21-Nov	13.11	1:34:46	7:14	**8.30**	Training half marathon
24-Nov	3.11	25:10	8:06	7.41	
26-Nov	4.01	28:27	7:06	8.46	
28-Nov	4.29	29:44	6:56	8.65	
1-Dec	2.5	19:00	7:36	7.89	Treadmill
5-Dec	8.00	56:33	7:04	8.49	
8-Dec	5.50	38:06	6:56	8.66	
15-Dec	4.25	35:09	8:16	7.25	Treadmill, speed and incline
20-Dec	2.13	17:29	8:12	7.31	
22-Dec	8.00	55:08	6:54	8.71	
25-Dec	7.00	54:28	7:47	7.71	
27-Dec	4.01	27:16	6:48	8.82	
29-Dec	12.00	1:30:51	7:34	7.93	

2014 Running / Race Log (Page 1)

Date	(Miles) Distance	Time	Pace Min / Mile	MPH	Notes
5-Jan	4.50	36:35	8:08	7.38	Treadmill, intervals
12-Jan	8.38	1:00:00	7:10	8.38	
16-Jan	3.53	24:43	7:00	8.57	
19-Jan	6.29	44:58	7:09	8.39	
26-Jan	7.14	50:28	7:04	8.49	
2-Feb	3.00	21:47	7:16	8.26	Treadmill, intervals
6-Feb	3.00	20:23	6:48	8.83	Treadmill, intervals
9-Feb	5.00	35:59	7:12	8.34	
13-Feb	5.00	35:24	7:05	8.47	
16-Feb	5.00	38:55	7:47	7.71	Treadmill, intervals and incline
20-Feb	9.12	1:08:22	7:30	8.00	
23-Feb	9.12	1:06:59	7:21	8.17	
27-Feb	4.69	35:00	7:28	8.04	
2-Mar	6.00	46:43	7:47	7.71	
4-Mar	2.06	15:02	7:18	8.22	
6-Mar	7.50	55:31	7:24	8.11	10 degrees - why am I outdoors?
9-Mar	10.07	1:13:25	7:17	8.23	
11-Mar	4.01	27:01	6:44	8.91	Including first 5k at 20:28
17-Mar	4.11	29:48	7:15	8.28	
18-Mar	5.25	36:38	6:59	8.60	
20-Mar	12	1:29:27	7:27	8.05	
25-Mar	4.57	35:48	7:50	7.66	
27-Mar	10	1:11:43	7:10	8.37	Pretty windy, close to 10 mile PB
30-Mar	5.00	33:48	6:46	8.88	New shoes, 5k in 19:53
1-Apr	4.42	36:27	8:15	7.28	
3-Apr	13.11	1:38:01	7:29	8.03	Windy, first "half" of 2014
6-Apr	6.00	42:00	7:00	8.57	
8-Apr	3.50	31:57	9:08	6.57	Boston, at a conference
11-Apr	10	1:09:59	6:60	**8.57**	10 miles under 7.00!
13-Apr	6.00	47:35	7:56	7.57	
17-Apr	7	47:39	6:48	**8.81**	
18-Apr	3.11	21:39	6:58	8.62	
20-Apr	8.19	59:59	7:19	8.19	
23-Apr	4.01	25:59	6:29	**9.26**	Windy, first 5k in 20:08
25-Apr	13.11	1:36:21	7:21	8.16	
27-Apr	8.00	58:55	7:22	8.15	
28-Apr	4.25	34:55	8:13	7.30	Intervals, including 1:22
1-May	8.00	57:12	7:09	8.39	
4-May	13.3	1:36:32	7:20	**8.18**	Novi Half marathon
6-May	5.01	34:01	6:47	8.84	
8-May	8.00	55:36	6:57	8.63	
9-May	3.38	27:44	8:12	7.31	
11-May	3.50	22:53	6:32	9.18	last 5k in 19:52
11-May	2.50	17:31	7:00	8.56	
13-May	6.22	45:12	7:16	8.26	
15-May	13.11	1:34:11	7:11	8.35	Half PB (at the time)
16-May	2.01	15:02	7:29	8.02	
18-May	3.16	19:49	6:16	**9.57**	Groves 5k, First official sub 20:00!
18-May	2.01	15:44	7:50	7.67	
20-May	6.01	46:40	7:46	7.73	Intervals, including 1:17

2014 Running / Race Log (Page 2)

Date	(Miles) Distance	Time	Pace Min / Mile	MPH	Notes
22-May	10.30	1:12:47	7:04	**8.49**	
23-May	3.00	22:30	7:30	8.00	
25-May	1.00	7:00	7:00	8.57	
26-May	6.3	41:36	6:36	**9.09**	Novi Memorial Day 10k
27-May	8.65	1:03:53	7:23	8.12	Hot, humid, hills, afternoon
29-May	8.48	59:59	7:04	8.48	
30-May	3.26	29:31	9:03	6.63	Intervals, light
1-Jun	13.24	1:35:02	7:11	**8.36**	Dexter Ann Arbor half
1-Jun	2.01	19:33	9:44	6.17	Light run after Dexter
3-Jun	6.13	48:21	7:53	7.61	Intervals, 1:18, some 800s
6-Jun	6.50	44:39	6:52	8.73	
8-Jun	3.06	19:13	6:17	**9.55**	Scleroderma 5k #1 overall!
8-Jun	1.61	11:07	6:54	8.69	light run after 5k
11-Jun	10.01	1:10:55	7:05	8.47	
13-Jun	5.80	44:10	7:37	7.88	
15-Jun	26.20	3:28:56	7:58	7.52	Marathon distance - tried it!
17-Jun	6.22	43:18	6:58	8.62	
19-Jun	6.01	44:23	7:23	8.12	
22-Jun	3.51	23:49	6:47	8.84	With Daughter on Rollerblades!
22-Jun	4.50	35:59	7:60	7.50	Intervals / fartleks, mostly 800s
24-Jun	3.11	19:41	6:20	9.48	Practice 5k, followed by light 2
24-Jun	2.01	14:27	7:11	8.35	
26-Jun	7.01	47:49	6:49	8.80	close to PB for 7 miles
27-Jun	5.30	37:46	7:08	8.42	
29-Jun	1.01	7:13	7:09	8.40	
29-Jun	5.01	35:35	7:06	8.45	
1-Jul	13.10	1:34:28	7:13	8.32	
6-Jul	4.60	33:30	7:17	8.24	Estimated
9-Jul	0.60	4:30	7:30	8.00	
9-Jul	8.01	54:21	6:47	**8.84**	PB for 8 miles
11-Jul	6.22	42:33	6:50	8.77	
13-Jul	3.16	26:45	8:28	7.09	Interals, mostly 400s, 1:23-1:27 range
13-Jul	3.14	21:55	6:59	8.60	With Daughter on Rollerblades!
16-Jul	3.11	19:41	6:19	9.49	Practice 5k
17-Jul	9.33	1:05:47	7:03	8.51	
18-Jul	5.30	35:46	6:45	8.89	
20-Jul	8.75	1:04:25	7:22	8.15	Hills
22-Jul	5.01	41:06	8:12	7.31	Intervals
24-Jul	13.11	1:32:22	7:03	**8.52**	Half PB (at the time)
25-Jul	3.40	29:00	8:32	7.03	Intervals
27-Jul	5.02	33:07	6:36	**9.10**	Electric Bolt 8k (PB)
29-Jul	6.22	43:32	6:60	8.57	Intervals, First mile in 5:53
30-Jul	3.11	19:41	6:20	9.48	Training 5k
31-Jul	10.0	1:09:52	6:59	**8.59**	10 miles under 7.00! Last mile 6:38
1-Aug	3.50	24:35	7:01	8.54	
3-Aug	3.11	19:04	6:08	**9.79**	PB 5k (right after a speeding ticket!)
3-Aug	1.71	28:52	16:53	3.55	
4-Aug	2.01	12:34	6:15	9.60	
6-Aug	6.22	41:49	6:43	8.92	
8-Aug	9.01	1:03:51	7:05	8.47	

2014 Running / Race Log (Page 3)

Date	(Miles) Distance	Time	Pace Min / Mile	MPH	Notes
10-Aug	4.53	37:19	8:14	7.28	Intervals
11-Aug	3.30	23:43	7:11	8.35	
14-Aug	7.00	47:12	6:45	**8.90**	7 Mile PB (at the time)
14-Aug	1.07	12:41	11:51	5.06	with my kid
17-Aug	5.05	37:59	7:31	7.98	Intervals
19-Aug	6.22	39:51	6:24	**9.37**	10k PB (unofficial). 19:36, then 20:15
21-Aug	11.50	1:19:59	6:57	**8.63**	11.5 miles PB
22-Aug	0.80	5:45	7:11	8.35	
22-Aug	3.00	21:11	7:04	8.50	
24-Aug	3.11	19:21	6:13	9.64	Training 5k
26-Aug	7.01	46:37	6:39	**9.02**	7 Mile PB (at the time)
28-Aug	13.11	1:31:26	6:58	**8.60**	PB half
30-Aug	3.80	26:06	6:52	8.74	
31-Aug	5.01	39:40	7:55	7.58	Intervals
1-Sep	6.22	42:51	6:53	8.71	Hills
2-Sep	3.11	19:27	6:15	9.59	Training 5k
4-Sep	10.00	1:08:23	6:50	**8.77**	
7-Sep	5.54	43:12	7:48	7.69	Intervals
9-Sep	6.22	42:03	6:46	8.88	First mile 5:47! PB
10-Sep	3.01	21:59	7:18	8.22	Intervals
11-Sep	9.04	1:00:01	6:38	**9.04**	Fastest 9 miles, and hour run!
14-Sep	3.22	19:34	6:05	**9.87**	5k Run Wild at Detroit Zoo, PB Speed!
14-Sep	6.35	42:01	6:37	9.07	10k, Run Wild at Detroit Zoo after 5k
16-Sep	4.16	33:05	7:57	7.54	Intervals
17-Sep	13.11	1:33:09	7:06	8.44	Decent, but low energy last 4 miles
19-Sep	4.94	32:30	6:35	9.12	
21-Sep	5.27	42:48	8:07	7.39	
23-Sep	8.00	53:22	6:40	8.99	
29-Sep	6.70	46:02	6:52	8.73	
30-Sep	3.60	32:00	8:53	6.75	
2-Oct	11.00	1:16:28	6:57	**8.63**	
5-Oct	6.65	46:24	6:59	8.60	Hills
7-Oct	8.01	58:49	7:21	8.17	Intervals for 3, then another 5 miles
8-Oct	3.11	19:32	6:17	9.55	Training 5k
12-Oct	7.01	49:54	7:07	8.43	
13-Oct	3.01	22:40	7:32	7.97	Intervals
15-Oct	7.01	46:22	6:37	**9.07**	Solid 7
19-Oct	13.26	1:32:20	6:58	**8.62**	Free Press half, Estimated distance
22-Oct	3.11	20:28	6:35	9.12	Training 5k
23-Oct	2.50	15:58	6:23	9.39	
26-Oct	9.00	1:07:01	7:27	8.06	Easy
28-Oct	4.72	30.01	6:22	**9.43**	30 minute PB
30-Oct	9.01	1:02:34	6:57	8.64	Fartleks
2-Nov	8.00	51.58	6:30	**9.24**	8 mile PB
4-Nov	10.35	1:15:00	7:15	8.28	Easy
6-Nov	6.15	44:58	7:19	8.21	Intervals
9-Nov	6.3	39:55	6:20	**9.47**	Big Bird 10k PB Under 40:00!
13-Nov	6.35	42:42	6:43	8.92	
16-Nov	1.26	10:00	7:56	7.56	Treadmill
20-Nov	2.10	17:00	8:06	7.41	Treadmill, 5:50 mile, some incline

2014 Running / Race Log (Page 4)					
	(Miles)		Pace		
Date	**Distance**	**Time**	**Min / Mile**	**MPH**	**Notes**
23-Nov	6.01	40:27	6:44	8.91	
26-Nov	5.25	35:15	6:43	8.94	Fartleks
28-Nov	3.00	26:00	8:40	6.92	
30-Nov	18.01	2:16:49	7:36	7.90	Distance training
4-Dec	5.60	36:54	6:35	9.11	
7-Dec	5.37	37:17	6:57	8.64	
9-Dec	4.01	25:31	6:22	9.43	Solid 4 miles
11-Dec	1.00	7:58	7:58	7.53	
14-Dec	9.25	1:07:06	7:15	8.27	Easy, long run
21-Dec	6.22	41:36	6:41	8.97	
26-Dec	3.11	23:00	7:24	8.11	

2015 Running / Race Log (Page 1)

	(Miles)		Pace		
Date	**Distance**	**Time**	**Min / Mile**	**MPH**	
4-Jan	12.25	1:31:11	7:27	8.06	long run training
7-Jan	2.00	14:54	7:27	8.05	treadmill, intervals
9-Jan	1.50	9:42	6:28	9.28	treadmill
11-Jan	8.57	59:16	6:55	8.68	indoor track
14-Jan	2.50	19:57	7:59	7.52	treadmill intervals
15-Jan	2.55	19:05	7:29	8.02	treadmill incline
18-Jan	11.80	1:26:35	7:20	8.18	long run training
22-Jan	3.00	22:55	7:38	7.85	treadmill fartleks
23-Jan	4.40	30:01	6:49	8.80	
25-Jan	10.11	1:16:56	7:37	7.88	long run training
27-Jan	2.00	15:39	7:50	7.67	treadmill intervals and incline
28-Jan	5.01	33:39	6:43	8.93	
1-Feb	4.00	30:30	7:38	7.87	treadmill intervals and incline
5-Feb	4.35	30:00	6:54	8.70	treadmill
8-Feb	17.00	2:07:45	7:31	7.98	long run training
10-Feb	1.00	6:06	6:06	9.84	treadmill, speed
11-Feb	4.01	25:48	6:26	9.33	First 5k at 19:45
15-Feb	8.00	53:25	6:41	**8.99**	
17-Feb	1.54	12:00	7:48	7.70	treadmill
20-Feb	1.55	13:00	8:23	7.15	treadmill
22-Feb	17.01	2:06:45	7:27	8.05	long run training
25-Feb	3.29	25:00	7:36	7.90	treadmill, intervals
27-Feb	1.81	15:00	8:17	7.24	treadmill, incline
1-Mar	6.09	40:00	6:34	9.14	
3-Mar	5.15	35:00	6:48	8.83	
8-Mar	18.01	2:15:54	7:33	7.95	long run training
11-Mar	3.70	26:56	7:17	8.24	
13-Mar	5.20	36:02	6:56	8.66	fartleks
15-Mar	10.01	1:13:42	7:22	8.15	
18-Mar	7.01	49:02	6:60	8.58	
20-Mar	3.22	23:45	7:23	8.13	
22-Mar	17.00	2:12:40	7:48	7.69	long run training
24-Mar	4.26	33:00	7:45	7.75	intervals
26-Mar	8.00	55:28	6:56	8.65	
29-Mar	8.25	1:02:23	7:34	7.93	
31-Mar	2.51	18:26	7:21	8.17	
2-Apr	20.00	2:34:38	7:44	7.76	Final marathon training
6-Apr	2.50	15:49	6:20	9.48	
7-Apr	2.06	19:42	9:34	6.27	Ran with one of the kids
8-Apr	10.00	1:13:25	7:21	8.17	
12-Apr	12.55	1:33:29	7:27	8.05	
14-Apr	4.19	33:44	8:03	7.45	Intervals, including a 1:20
15-Apr	4.42	35:10	7:57	7.54	Easy 8 AM
15-Apr	3.01	29:50	9:55	6.05	Ran with one of the kids
17-Apr	8.01	54:31	6:48	8.82	
19-Apr	8.18	1:01:20	7:30	8.00	Morning food same as marathon
21-Apr	4.88	37:44	7:44	7.76	Intervals
22-Apr	4.12	31:28	7:38	7.86	
24-Apr	1.09	10:00	9:10	6.54	Minimal effort
26-Apr	26.44	3:23:49	7:43	7.78	Glass City Marathon!

2015 Running / Race Log (Page 2)

	(Miles)		Pace		
Date	**Distance**	**Time**	**Min / Mile**	**MPH**	
28-Apr	2.75	22:07	8:03	7.46	Easy run, pretty stiff!
29-Apr	5.00	37:47	7:33	7.94	Easy
1-May	3.21	22:01	6:52	8.75	
3-May	4.16	30:29	7:20	8.19	
5-May	5.77	47:23	8:13	7.31	
7-May	9.25	1:02:40	6:46	8.86	
10-May	3.13	19:43	6:18	9.52	Training 5k
10-May	3.41	25:08	7:22	8.14	
12-May	3.11	19:44	6:21	9.46	Training 5k
12-May	3.00	21:05	7:02	8.54	
14-May	10.35	1:14:43	7:13	8.31	
15-May	3.00	24:00	8:00	7.50	
17-May	3.16	19:32	6:11	9.71	Groves Orchestra 5k, #3!
18-May	12.01	1:25:40	7:08	8.41	
19-May	3.43	23:27	6:50	8.78	
21-May	9.01	1:04:41	7:11	8.36	Hills
22-May	2.01	15:06	7:31	7.99	Track
22-May	1.01	6:13	6:09	9.75	last mile on track
26-May	7.01	47:57	6:50	8.77	Fartleks
28-May	8.01	55:24	6:55	8.68	
29-May	0.77	5:39	7:20	8.18	Track segment
29-May	1.49	11:01	7:24	8.11	Track segment
29-May	1.02	7:27	7:18	8.21	Track segment
31-May	13.24	1:33:18	7:03	8.51	Dexter Ann Arbor
2-Jun	5.01	36:51	7:21	8.16	Intervals
4-Jun	8.65	1:00:01	6:56	8.65	
5-Jun	3.36	24:00	7:09	8.40	
7-Jun	3.1	18:51	6:05	**9.87**	Scleroderma 5k, PB
7-Jun	2.01	13:34	6:45	8.89	
9-Jun	7.66	54:02	7:03	8.51	
11-Jun	8.01	56:34	7:04	8.50	
12-Jun	4.50	31:00	6:53	8.71	
14-Jun	2.00	11:59	5:60	**10.01**	2 miles under 12:00!!
15-Jun	3.40	25:00	7:21	8.16	
17-Jun	4.01	25:40	6:24	9.37	
18-Jun	4.76	33:54	7:07	8.42	
19-Jun	4.00	28:00	7:00	8.57	
21-Jun	6.34	46:22	7:19	8.20	
23-Jun	8.59	1:00:23	7:02	8.54	
25-Jun	2.07	17:14	8:20	7.21	
26-Jun	5.01	37:41	7:31	7.98	
28-Jun	6.50	47:11	7:16	8.27	
30-Jun	10.00	1:06:31	6:39	**9.02**	10 mile personal best
2-Jul	6.00	44:54	7:29	8.02	
3-Jul	3.04	19:03	6:16	9.57	Oak Park Mayor's 5k, #1!
3-Jul	3.11	22:30	7:14	8.29	
7-Jul	5.00	34:50	6:58	8.61	
9-Jul	7.00	48:07	6:52	8.73	
10-Jul	1.33	10:02	7:33	7.95	
10-Jul	2.36	15:43	6:40	9.01	

2015 Running / Race Log (Page 3)

Date	(Miles) Distance	Time	Pace Min / Mile	MPH	
12-Jul	5.00	37:30	7:30	8.00	
14-Jul	5.02	36:25	7:15	8.27	Fartleks
16-Jul	8.00	54:25	6:48	8.82	Early morning, solid 8 miles
17-Jul	3.68	25:27	6:55	8.68	
19-Jul	1.67	11:13	6:43	8.93	
21-Jul	4.50	28:23	6:18	**9.51**	training 5k and 19:31
22-Jul	5.00	35:55	7:11	8.35	
24-Jul	7.01	48:00	6:51	8.76	
28-Jul	13.11	1:29:58	6:52	8.74	PB half at the time
30-Jul	3.00	20:13	6:44	8.90	
31-Jul	5.61	41:39	7:25	8.08	
2-Aug	3.29	20:27	6:13	9.65	End Homelessness, #1
2-Aug	3.24	22:29	6:56	8.65	
4-Aug	5.01	35:01	6:59	8.58	
6-Aug	4.25	30:00	7:04	8.50	Intervals, including a 5:43 Mile!
9-Aug	8.00	1:04:00	11:08	5.39	
13-Aug	5.01	35:20	7:03	8.51	
14-Aug	6.50	44:00	6:46	8.86	
16-Aug	4.01	30:31	7:37	7.88	Intervals
18-Aug	4.00	25:41	6:25	9.34	
19-Aug	5.00	35:03	7:01	8.56	
21-Aug	4.00	27:56	6:59	8.59	
23-Aug	16.01	1:56:50	7:18	8.22	"OK" 18 mile run
25-Aug	6.60	45:12	6:51	8.76	
27-Aug	8.00	55:20	6:55	8.67	
28-Aug	5.00	41:00	8:12	7.32	
31-Aug	6.00	42:00	7:00	8.57	
3-Sep	8.50	57:37	6:47	8.85	New watch, hills, solid splits
4-Sep	3.50	24:40	7:03	8.51	
7-Sep	3.13	21:25	6:51	8.77	With kid on rollerblades
8-Sep	4.00	26:06	6:32	9.20	training first 5k 19:50
10-Sep	13.11	**1:28:56**	6:47	**8.84**	PB half
11-Sep	4.18	31:25	7:31	7.98	
13-Sep	2.50	19:11	7:40	7.82	
17-Sep	6.50	44:35	6:52	8.75	Fartlek miles for 2, 4, and 6
18-Sep	4.75	31:45	6:41	8.98	
20-Sep	5.65	39:35	7:00	8.56	Incline / Hills
22-Sep	4.50	30:24	6:45	8.88	
24-Sep	5.01	34:34	6:54	8.70	Intervals
25-Sep	5.10	36:33	7:10	8.37	
27-Sep	11.50	1:22:18	7:09	8.38	
30-Sep	7.00	45:14	6:28	**9.29**	Solid tempo 7 miles
2-Oct	5.75	38:39	6:43	8.93	
4-Oct	5.5	40:20	7:20	8.18	
8-Oct	9.05	1:01:00	6:44	8.90	
9-Oct	4.27	34:50	8:09	7.36	
11-Oct	8	55:00	6:53	8.73	
13-Oct	4.4	30:42	6:59	8.60	Intervals
15-Oct	6.00	40:31	6:45	8.89	Easy 6 prior to half
16-Oct	2.60	18:41	7:11	8.35	

2015 Running / Race Log (Page 4)

	(Miles)		Pace		
Date	Distance	Time	Min / Mile	MPH	
18-Oct	13.31	1:29:45	6:45	**8.90**	Detroit US half, under 1:30!!!
20-Oct	3.80	26:54	7:05	8.48	
22-Oct	6.01	40:42	6:46	8.86	
23-Oct	4.91	37:17	7:36	7.90	
25-Oct	5.70	38:11	6:42	8.96	
27-Oct	4.12	26:26	6:25	9.35	First 5k at 20:02, negative splits
29-Oct	7.50	51:47	6:54	8.69	
30-Oct	2.00	14:26	7:13	8.31	
1-Nov	3.11	18:52	6:04	**9.89**	Very solid training 5K
3-Nov	6.50	43:30	6:42	8.97	
5-Nov	9.00	1:01:45	6:52	8.74	
8-Nov	5.00	31:13	6:15	**9.61**	Very solid 5 miles, PB
11-Nov	10.00	1:08:25	6:51	8.77	
13-Nov	5.00	33:14	6:39	9.03	Mile Fartleks
15-Nov	5.50	41:03	7:28	8.04	
17-Nov	8.00	53:29	6:41	8.97	
19-Nov	7.30	51:10	7:01	8.56	no hydration
20-Nov	2.00	14:30	7:15	8.28	treamill, speed workout
22-Nov	3.00	23:12	7:44	7.76	
23-Nov	1.25	12:13	9:46	6.14	treamill, incline workout
24-Nov	6.50	44:27	6:50	8.77	
26-Nov	6.31	39:19	6:14	**9.63**	Turkey Trot, 10k PB!!!
29-Nov	1.62	16:10	9:59	6.01	
1-Dec	1.75	16:10	9:14	6.49	
3-Dec	1.76	16:00	9:05	6.60	
4-Dec	5.56	36:28	6:34	9.15	
6-Dec	3.11	25:27	8:11	7.33	
8-Dec	2.41	16:39	6:55	8.68	
10-Dec	6.00	39:56	6:39	9.02	
13-Dec	4.63	30:00	6:29	9.26	Solid 30 minutes
15-Dec	1.61	15:30	9:38	6.23	
17-Dec	7.55	50:51	6:44	8.91	
20-Dec	6.43	43:20	6:44	8.90	indoor track
24-Dec	11.00	1:16:50	6:59	8.59	
25-Dec	4.50	29:50	6:38	9.05	
27-Dec	3.05	30:00	9:50	6.10	
30-Dec	3.00	24:55	8:18	7.22	
31-Dec	12.00	1:23:00	6:55	8.67	

Printed by Amazon Italia Logistica S.r.l.
Torrazza Piemonte (TO), Italy